HOW TO DECIPHER
DOCUMENTS.

How to read
Old Documents
E. E. Thoyts

with an introduction by
C. TRICE MARTIN

Phillimore

First published in 1893
Reprinted 1972, 1980

Published by
PHILLIMORE & CO. LTD.
Shopwyke Manor Barn, Chichester, West Sussex

Reprinted in paperback 2001

© Phillimore & Co. Ltd., 1980, 2001

ISBN 1 86077 172 6

Printed and bound in Great Britain by
BIDDLES LTD.
Guildford, Surrey

INTRODUCTION.

B OOKS written to teach any branch of human knowledge are, in most cases, written by persons who have long known and used the knowledge which they impart, and, perhaps for that reason, have more or less forgotten the steps of the ladder up which they have climbed ; but in this case the process has been so recent, that the difficulties and dangers of each step have been remembered, and the reader accordingly warned against them.

The meaning of the various kinds of documents which are likely to be found among the title-deeds of an estate, or among the archives of a parish or a corporation, are described without needless technicalities, in a practical way, which will appeal to those who begin to work among such material without previous knowledge.

The first step, of course, is to learn to read. This wants perseverance and a quick eye, but regular practice will soon enable the student to read any ordinary documents, which at first seemed utterly unintelligible, and gradually the power of understanding really difficult and obscure MSS. will be acquired. But this first step must be thoroughly mastered, for to attempt to get information from old writings without thoroughly knowing the forms of the letters, and the different systems of abbreviations and contractions, would be like trying to keep accounts without knowing how to add up a column of figures.

And indeed paleography is the foundation of all history. There may be historians, like the late Mr. Freeman, who have but little knowledge of the science (he, I believe, boasted of his inability to read a manuscript), but then such writers rely on the paleographic knowledge of others, who have edited the manuscripts which they desire to use, and they have, or ought to have, sufficient scholarship to judge which are the best editions, and even occasionally to detect editors' mistakes.

But an acquaintance with this branch of knowledge is often of the greatest use to biographers and historians. It is much better, for instance, to be able to judge whether a certain document is of the age which it professes, or in whose hand a draft of a treaty is, than to have to accept the opinion of someone else.

The mistakes made for want of this knowledge are common, and sometimes very amusing. Familiar enough is the old story of the parish priest in the time of King Henry VIII., who in the canon of the Mass, in the prayer after taking the wine, read the word: *sumpsimus*, as *mumpsimus*, because he had a thirteenth-century missal in which *s* and *m* are much alike, and refused to alter his mistake when it was pointed out to him. It was referred to by King Henry VIII. in his speech to the Parliament in 1545, and, in fact, this ignorant priest has ' made himself an everlasting name' for conservative stupidity.

In more recent times, the historian of one of our beautiful north-country abbeys talks of a gift of a silver chest by the founder in the eleventh century. The reader wonders what this chest could have been—was it a native work or imported? was it some ecclesiastical ornament or merely a strong box? But on turning to the document on which the account is based, the meaning is clear. It was not a chest of silver, but an ordinary mark of silver. The MS. reads *unāmarcāargenti*. The writer of the book had

not noticed the contraction over the first *a*,
divided the words wrongly, and read it *unam
arcam*, instead of *unam marcam*.

In another similar book the story is narrated
of the ill-treatment by a forester of an abbot
whose house was near a royal forest. The abbot
was no doubt like the monk who made the celebrated pilgrimage to Canterbury—

> ' An outrydere that lovede venerye.
>
>   *   *   *   *   *
>
> He yaf nat of that text a pulled hen
> That seith that hunters been nat holy men.'

And perhaps the forester had good reason to com-
plain of him. But in the account of the quarrel,
the forester is said to have gone into the abbot's
kitchen and taken away his cabbages—not very
likely things for a forester to take, as he probably
would have found something far better worth
carrying off. However, on looking at the MS. it
appears almost certain that what was read as
chous is really *chens*, that is, *chiens*. In fact, they
were the

> ' Grehoundes he hadde as swifte as fowel in flight,
> For priking and for hunting for the hare,'

who were perhaps lying before the fire asleep after
a long afternoon's coursing.

In the same case it is said that the forester's
treatment of the tenants on one of the abbey
farms is so bad that no one dare die there; it is

suggested, because the forester would not allow anyone to come to administer the last consolations of religion. But the words *de murir*, on which the observation is based, are merely a careless scribe's writing of *demeurer*.

In another book farmers are represented as using stones for fuel, which are suggested to have been coal; but this results from misreading *petarum* (peat), as if it were *pet^{a}rum*, a contracted form of *petrarum* (stones).

The spreading desire to know something of paleography is very remarkable, and is much to be commended. For all persons who interest themselves in the documents to which they may have access in the possession of private persons, or in repositories not generally known, are helping in the grand work of making clear the laws and customs and mode of living of our ancestors, and thus constantly come across information, not to be found in our more public collections of records, which often throws light on many dark passages of history.

C. T. MARTIN.

AUTHOR'S PREFACE.

I N the following pages I have tried to describe the things which puzzled me when, as a beginner, I first essayed to read and understand the old records of bygone times. Written in a language I knew not, relating to customs no longer existing, all was strange and unfamiliar. I toiled on; by degrees light dawned and the difficulties melted away. The knowledge thus gained I have endeavoured, in all humility, to write down as a possible guide and help to others who may, like myself, prefer to follow antiquarian research by means of old deeds and other manuscripts, as being the original source and most trustworthy fountain-head of knowledge, and by this means to avoid as much as possible repeating the assertions and mistakes of previous writers.

In the chapter on Paleography I have named

the books which were my guides, and in these pages I have tried to supply information supplementary to what is already printed on the subject, rather than repeat what has previously been explained. The growing fashion for all kinds of antiquarianism creates a desire for books treating upon such subjects, and this has induced me to write this book.

E. E. THOYTS.

SULHAMSTEAD, *May*, 1893.

CONTENTS.

LIST OF ILLUSTRATIONS.

ERRATA.

Page 77, line 2, *for* ' miniscule ' *read* ' minuscule.'
,, 85, line 4, *for* ' single ' *read* ' one or more.'
,, 89, line 17, *for* ' mendicant orders ' *read* ' mendicants.'
,, 89, line 26, *for* ' 1219 ' *read* ' 1204, and confirmed in 1215.'
,, 92, *for* ' Monumentæ Ritualiæ ' *read* ' Monumenta Ritualia.'
,, 93, *for* ' charter ' *read* ' cartulary.'

HOW TO DECIPHER AND STUDY OLD DOCUMENTS.

CHAPTER I.

HINTS TO BEGINNERS.

FASHION changes in everything; but these alterations go on so imperceptibly, so gradually, that ofttimes we fail to recognise their progress except by glancing backwards into the past. But the fashion of handwriting and its changes are very forcibly brought home to us when confronted for the first time with some old deed or paper; and a hopeless feeling of helplessness reduces the amateur to the verge or despair as the pages of unintelligible hieroglyphics are spread out, lacking in any sense, and as unfamiliar as Sanscrit or Egyptian characters. But perseverance conquers all difficulties.

Every generation has its own particular type

of writing. Compare, for instance, any bundle
of letters taken, hap-hazard, out of an old desk
or secrétaire; it is quite easy to sort them into
bundles in sequence of dates, and also guess
accurately the age and position of the writers.

The flowing Italian hand, used by educated
women early in this century, has changed with
fashion into the freer style of the succeeding
generation; this in the third generation has
further developed into the bold, decisive, almost
masculine writing adopted by the more strong-
minded females of the latter end of this nineteenth century.

Of course, school-teaching is responsible to a
certain extent for a set handwriting. Our Univer-
sity men of to-day all, with few exceptions, use
a neat scholarly form of writing, free from
flourishes, and with simple capital letters and
the small broken-backed Greek letter *s*. Compared with the scholar's, the soldier's writing
is bolder and rounder, while the clerk's is still
more distinct in type in its open lettering, interspersed with curls and twists. So with most
professions it will be found that each has special
characteristics; but these are liable to change
according to circumstances; thus, the clerk will
form his letters less distinctly after the need of
great legibility no longer compels him to carefulness. Self-education will often alter a vulgar

ill-formed writing to a better, more studied style ; and writing is the clearest proof of both bodily and mental condition, for in cases of paralysis or mental aberration the doctor takes it as a certain guide.

Looking back to the days when writing was a profession of itself, it can easily be understood how it is that we find less variety among old writings. For in those days, before printing was discovered, or at least but imperfectly executed and understood, all books had to be produced by hand, and were the work either of paid scribes, whose duty it was to reproduce copies of well-known authors; or else copied out by clerks or private secretaries at the dictation of the authors themselves, who could seldom spare the time to commit their ideas to paper, or, even if they did so, it was customary to have additional copies made by professed scribes. Unacquainted with the subjects of the books, and copying merely from verbal dictation, it is no wonder that mistakes and misunderstandings often occurred, especially in the spelling of place and personal names; for one man reading aloud to several scribes, each would write down the names and words as they sounded to his individual sense of hearing, for the constant interruption necessary to ensure complete accuracy would cause the process to be tedious and very lengthy.

Private correspondence, even, was carried on as a profession; writing shops existed up to a comparatively late period.

Authors who wrote their own books had them afterwards transcribed neatly for preservation, and probably destroyed the original notes, for of these comparatively few, if any, exist.

All the earliest writers had a special education for their profession, being sent to some monastery for that purpose; hence they were either foreigners, or educated under foreign monks, either French or Italian, and the effect of this teaching is clearly demonstrated by the similitude which exists all over Europe between manuscripts of the early Middle Ages.

In England the Norman Conquest overruled most of the previous customs and styles. Vast crowds of Normans emigrated continuously to our shores. This went on more or less for at least three or four centuries, and then prejudice against foreigners asserted itself, and the Saxon element, which still remained among the lower classes of the people, gained the ascendant. In the reign of Henry V. alien priories were suppressed, and foreign monks and priests no longer travelled backwards and forwards from the Norman abbeys to the junior houses or cells in England. The rich merchants, who resorted here from the Low Countries and Germany, brought with them their own customs and fashions; and at this time will first be noticed the use of a written character, like the modern German, which steadily came more and more into use until the end of the seventeenth century, when it died out and the style altered to a rounder, freer hand.

So long as education was almost entirely monastic, or at least conducted by teachers trained in monastic institutions, we find (as we should naturally expect to do) a regularity, carefulness and formality in the handwriting of the period; but so soon as England had shaken off the authority of Rome and the educated communities had been scattered and disbanded, a marked change took place in all kinds of writing. The monks and nuns, rendered homeless by the Reformation, returned to their native villages, thus spreading education among all classes and creating a desire after learning. But the primary cause of the alteration in handwriting, so very marked in the sixteenth century, was perhaps attributable to the introduction of the art of printing, which naturally was fatal to handwriting as a profession. The scribe was no longer required to multiply the author's productions; so that lawyers and public office clerks only remained out of the large class who had formerly earned their living as professional writers. In the actual writing, also, a change took place. The

old elaborate letters were supplanted by the
simple capitals copied from the printer's blocks.
Some day, maybe, writing will die out altogether;
every year fresh improvements and inventions
are increasing; even now type-writers and multi-
plying machines are used in place of handwriting
in many offices.

A hundred years ago, very few if any of the
labourers could either read or write; even now, in
out-of-the-way country places, there exist a few
old people ignorant of these (to us) necessary arts.
The marriage registers of the last century prove
to us the ignorance of the country folk, for neither
the contracting parties nor their witnesses could
often write their names, and instead used either
some eccentric monogram bearing a faint resemblance to initials—a memory perhaps of a
bygone and very slight amount of teaching; or
oftener still we find in lieu of name the old
Christian cross, which has been in use by the
illiterate from Saxon times as a pledge of good
faith and consent.

Previous to the present century, all education
in country places was either nil or provided out
of the bounty of the squire or parson, the teacher
being some old ignorant person prevented by age
or bodily infirmity from pursuing active labour,
and whose qualifications were merely a smattering
of the 'three R's,' which, with plain sewing,

was the whole of his useful though scanty ré
pertoire. Children then were sent out to work at
the age of nine or ten years, and earlier if any-
body could be found to employ them. When once
placed out, they had no opportunities of gaining
further book knowledge, and soon forgot the little
they had learnt for want of practice or stimula-
tion, nor had they sufficient mental capacity to
study by themselves, except in very exceptional
cases of natural genius.

If this was the state of things within the
memory of those still alive, we can well believe
how very limited was the knowledge of handwriting some hundreds of years ago, and can
more fully understand that the scribe was a very
important personage, and took great pride in his
work.

It is very rare to find mistakes or erasures in
the lettering of old charters. Varieties of spelling
occur everywhere; a name is often found spelt
two or three different ways on the same page;
but this is easily explained if the work was
written from dictation, especially if pronounced
to or by a foreigner. Our English language is so
full of unexpected variations of spelling that
it is no wonder that names of people and places
suffered at the hands of a transcriber unacquainted
with the localities, and who merely wrote down
the words as they sounded to him. The actual

spelling of words remained fairly constant.   Certainly to us they look very curious, for English orthography has undergone innumerable changes; in course of time new words are being repeatedly coined, and old words alter not only in spelling, but also in meaning and significance.   If we wish for an example of Old English phraseology, we have our present version of the Bible—which, being translated into English in the seventeenth century, now sounds quaint, and in many parts the sense of the words is a matter of dispute. If it be compared with the Revised Version the changes which have taken place in the two past centuries become very evident.   All this must be borne in mind when the task of transcribing and translating old writing is undertaken, and allowance must be made for all such alterations both in style and spelling.

It has been said that a knowledge of Latin is indispensable to the would-be transcriber of old deeds; this is not really the case for ordinary antiquarian research, for the meaning can be discovered easily with only a very slight amount of instruction. Legal Latin consists so entirely of set forms that when once these forms are familiar to the reader, they are without any difficulty recognised, and are so little liable to any variations that they are easily rendered into English.   The most important points being a correct and accurate attention to the names of people and places, with the descriptions of the localities referred to. As the use of Latin for legal transactions almost entirely superseded the Norman-French language after the reign of Edward III. (although it is an open question whether deeds were not duplicated into the two languages), very few old deeds are met with in the latter language, and those few are usually so well written and very legible, that they can easily be understood with the help of a slight knowledge of modern French.

Indeed, a transcriber's work properly consists chiefly in correctly putting into modern handwriting the deeds which are only illegible to the uninitiated; in consequence, an actual acquaintance with the Latin grammar is less important than a correct eye, quick to note every minute difference in letters. Every stroke of the pen means something; bars or curves are the representatives of absent words or syllables, and are never dashed down hap-hazard or by accident. Therefore it is possible to understand the abbreviated portions correctly, although extension with absolute correctness can never be ensured without study of the language and a knowledge of its grammar.

One of the best methods of learning to read courthand, is first to devote a short time to the study of shorthand; any system will do, it being merely a means of training the eye and brain into speedily noticing small shades of difference, undetected except by comparison. For in all kinds of shorthand the least stroke or dot, or even a change in the position of a line, will entirely alter the spelling or meaning of a word.

Next, I would advise the careful study of an old deed, one of those written late in the seventeenth century or early in the eighteenth, because these deeds give the phraseology or form of sentences, and are often written in English in a fairly clear hand, freer from contractions than earlier manuscripts, and the beginner has so many new things to discover and learn that it is well to commence by not attempting too much at the first start. An acquaintance with the style of words used in legal language is a good groundwork to commence with. Spread out the parchment before you; never mind the fact that only a word or two, or even only a chance letter here and there catches your eye. Then set to work to compare the letters of the words you do know with the letters in other words which at the commencement looked so strange to you.

It was in this way that Egyptian hieroglyphics were first successfully studied.

Remember that consonants seldom come together; no word is formed without the help of one or more vowels; the final letter or letters more often supply a clue than the capital letter or beginning syllable, especially in the so-called courthands.

Beware of too imaginative guesses. Although this fault is easily remedied, still, it is better to spell a word out letter by letter, however unintelligible and depressing the result at first may be. It is so easy to take a name or word for granted, and an idea once seized upon is not quickly eradicated, and may bring about absurd results and deductions.

Do not ponder too long over a word which puzzles you, but go on, leaving gaps in your copy with a stroke underneath corresponding with or leaving sufficient space for the missing word. These spaces can then be filled in afterwards, when the general sense of the document has been mastered and the aspect of the particular style of writing has become familiar. Then it will be found that words hitherto seemingly unintelligible resolve themselves into readable form, and although apparently impossible to decipher at the first reading, later on they present no difficulty. A little practice and patience soon overcome the difficulties of the first start, and after that the progress is rapid.

To begin by learning a variety of old alphabets seems to me so much waste of time, although it would be a valuable groundwork to commence

with. The true alphabet for beginners lies in the
contracted words, whose missing portions must
be supplied by the reader from the few letters
given, which are often not even one connected
syllable, but instead merely one or two letters
out of the missing syllable clustered together.

The reason for this style of writing was to save
time and material. With use it grew into a complete system, a language of its own. At the time
it was penned, these contractions were no doubt
perfectly familiar to all, just as our modern
abbreviations are. Of these last there are more
contractions in use nowadays than would at
first be realized—our daily correspondence is full
of them; these may have originated from the
older system of contractions, and be relics of it,
still left lingering on.

A few examples of modern abbreviations will
not be out of place here, as showing that a contracted form of writing is not so very difficult or
extraordinary after all.

&, and, derived from the Latin *et ;* the second
example, which is still in use, can be traced in
very old documents from et, till gradually it
assumed its modern shape.

M^r, mister or master; S^r for sir was formerly
in common use.

C^o, company; Cie, *compagnie* (French); etc.,
the first three letters of the Latin word *etcetera.*

The words with, which, whereof, where, etc., were formerly abbreviated; also y^r for your, ye the, and many others now obsolete.

Pounds, shillings and pence we still designate by the Latin £ s. d.

The long word 'affectionate' is seldom written in full; so, too, with many other words there are recognised forms of contraction, and when this is borne in mind the abbreviations of old deeds appear in quite a different light, and we attack their difficulties with less dread of failure.

CHAPTER II.

HANDWRITING.

MANY books have been recently published on the subject of 'Character by Handwriting,' but they are not very descriptive in detail, although the theories and rules for character-describing by this means are both clear and decided.

It is now no longer the rule to teach children to write entirely by the aid of set copies, as was the case with our forefathers, who wrote after one approved pattern, which children copied as nearly as possible from the original set for them ; therefore characteristic peculiarities were longer in asserting themselves, and what is now considered a 'formed' handwriting was not developed till late in life.

There were, and still are, two divisions or classes of handwriting—the professional and the personal ; with the first the action was mechanical, and exhibits few, if any, traces of personality. Yet even in the oldest manuscripts there are certain defined characteristics plainly shown. The handwritings of historical and celebrated personages coincide to a remarkable degree with their known virtues and vices, as criticised and detailed by their biographers.

As the art of writing became general, its form varied more and more, becoming gradually less formal, and each person wrote as was easiest to himself. Education, as a rule, has a far from beneficial effect upon handwriting; an active brain creates ideas too fast to give the hand time to form the letters clearly, patiently and evenly, the matter, not the material, being to the writer of primary importance.

So, as study increased among all classes, writing degenerated from its originally clear, regular lettering into every style of penmanship.

Of course a child's writing resembles only the copy-book, of which it is supposed to be an exact imitation; soon, however, the round curves sharpen, the disconnected letters join without any breaks in the words; the even lines and distances are no longer so carefully measured and considered; eccentricities of style creep in, with sundry loops and twirls, giving the whole a grown-up appearance—a decided individuality of its own.

If the subject of handwriting as a test of

character is carefully studied it will be found that immediate circumstances greatly influence it: anxiety or great excitement of any kind, illness or any violent emotion, will for the moment greatly affect the writing. From handwriting the doctor can hazard an opinion as to the mental state of his patient. In all cases of paralysis the writing is temporarily affected, and the patient is usually at first deprived of the power of writing; when the mind recovers its consciousness and the muscles their strength, the power returns, but with a feebleness not formerly observed. Writing depends upon so many things—a firm grasp of the pen, a pliability of the muscles, clearness of vision and brain-power — even the writing-materials, pens, ink and paper, all make a difference. It is not strange, then, that with so many causes upon which it depends, writing should be an excellent test of temperament and bodily health.

Any school-teacher or head of a college through whose hands a large correspondence passes, usually contracts a habit of forming conclusions as to the mental and moral calibre of the writers, their social status and natural bias of disposition. A round, childish handwriting is said to show conceit and self-satisfaction. Ignorance and conceit are often closely linked together. The uneducated generally have a very good opinion of their own personal qualifications. The most youthful form of writing is not, therefore, indicative of talent or general capacity, and seldom shows any originality.

All needless flourishes and ornamentation are the result of egotism and vanity. But be it remembered that any virtue exaggerated at once becomes a fault; that whereas a little conceit is necessary to stimulate ambition, the same in too great excess becomes egotistic vanity. Genius is apt to over-estimate its own depth and originality, yet without any self-appreciation there is danger of a lack of effort; despair prevents perseverance, and is a bar to any success.

Excitability, hastiness, and impatience are all seen in the handwriting at a glance. A quick brain suggests words and sentences so fast, one upon another, that though the pen races along the page it cannot write down the ideas quickly enough to satisfy the author. With a calm, calculating disposition this frantic haste is neither known nor understood—such persons do not rush to conclusions, but ponder over every subject. Intuitive perception in the excitable person becomes judgment in a tranquil mind. Temper depends upon temperament. The crosses of the letter 't' are the index whereby to judge of it. If these strokes are regular through a whole page of writing, the writer may be assumed to have an even-placed temper; if dashed off at random—

quick short strokes, somewhat higher than the letter itself — quick outbursts of anger may be expected, but of short duration, unless the stroke is firm and black, in which case great violence may safely be predicted.

Uncertainty of character and temper is shown by the variation of these strokes to the letter 't'. Sometimes the cross is firm and black, then next time it is light; sometimes it is omitted altogether, varying with each repetition of the letter like the opinions and sentiments of an undecided person. The up and down strokes of the letters tell of strength or weakness of will; gradations of light and shade, too, may be observed in these strokes. The sloping Italian handwriting of our grandmothers is just what might be expected from women refined and sensitive, grounded in several branches of study, well educated as a whole, but not especially so in any one particular line. The absence of any self-assertion is very strongly marked. The independence of their granddaughters can be traced in every line and stroke of their pens. Little or no distinction is observable between the writing of young men and women nowadays. Even the graphologist dare scarcely hazard an opinion as to the sex of the writer, but indulges in vague wording, avoiding any direct use of personal pronouns.

Capital letters tell us many points of interest.

By them originality, talent, and mental capacity
are displayed, as well as any latent vulgarity or
want of education. There are two styles of
capital letters at present in use. The high-class
style employed by persons of education is plain
and often eccentric, but without much ornamentation. The other may be called the middle-
class, for it is used by servants and tradespeople
having a fair amount of education, mingled with
a good deal of conceited ignorance and false pride.
With these last the capital letters are much

adorned by loops, hooks, and curves, noticeable
principally in the heads of the letters or at their
commencement. Perhaps, for purposes of character delineation, it will be better to give the
characteristics, pointing out the style and form
of the letters peculiar to each.

It will generally be found that with writing
having much resemblance, a characteristic simi-
larity also exists ; therefore, to become proficient
as a graphologist, a careful study must be made
of the writings of those whose whole life and

character, together with personal peculiarities, are intimately known and understood, and from this, conclusions may be drawn and rules arrived at for future use.

Affection is marked by open loops and a general slant or slope of the writing. A hard nature, unsympathetic and unimpressionable, has very little artistic feeling or love of the fine arts; therefore the same things which indicate a soft, affectionate disposition will also indicate poetry, music, and painting, or one or other kindred subjects. The first of these accompanies a loving, impulsive nature; with music the impulse is replaced by perseverance; for natural genius cannot expand without patient study. In painting three things are absolutely necessary to produce an artist. Form, colour, light and shade—all these three will influence the writing; but art of any kind is very complex. Success implies a certain degree of ambition, and consequent upon it is vanity and egotism; hence the artist's signature is generally peculiar and often unreadable, from its originality, egotism, and exuberance of creative power.

Imagination and impulse do not tend to improve handwriting. The strokes are too erratic, and the capital letters never follow the copybook pattern. Over-haste is visible in every line. A warm-hearted, impulsive person feels deeply and passionately at the moment of writing, and dashes off the words without regard to the effect they will produce upon the reader. What is generally lacking, is judgment and the power of analytical thought. These important qualities may be detected in disjoined words, which here and there may be seen even with a handwriting in which impulse and sequence of ideas are leading characteristics. The writer has evidently paused to think, although unaware of it himself. These breaks give a power of criticism, combined with clearness of intellect. Without breaks no commonsense is found, but if they appear too often it shows a wearying and needless worry over trivial details, and self-torment as to the opinions of other people.

Truth and straightforwardness give even lines running across the page and regular distances from one word to another. Tact is very essential. This quality requires often slight deceptions to be allowed or practised, white lies, or delusive silence; hence an unevenness in the writing is observed. It is a deviation, although slight, from the path of truth, and here and there the letters rise or fall below the lines. Untruthfulness gives greater unevenness still; but do not rush to conclusions on this point, for an unformed handwriting shows this peculiarity very often, being merely due, not to evil qualities, but to an unsteady hand employed in work to which it is unused.

Very round even writing in which the vowels are not closed, denotes candour and openness of disposition, with an aptitude for giving advice, whether asked or unasked, not always of a complimentary kind. Blunt, crabbed writing suggests obstinacy and a selfish love of power, without thought for the feelings of others. True selfishness gives every curve an inward bend, very marked in the commencement of words or capital letters.

Perseverance and patience are closely allied. In the former the letter ' t ' is hooked at the top, and also its stroke has a dark curved end, showing that when once an idea has been entertained no earthly persuasion will alter or eradicate it. Such writers have strongly-defined prejudices, and are apt to take very strong dislikes without much cause.

Calmness and patience also are frequently linked together—more often in later life, when adversity has blunted the faculties, or the dull routine of uneventful existence has destroyed all romance. Then the writing has short up-and-down strokes, the curves are round, the bars short and straight; there are no loops or flourishes; the whole writing exhibits great neatness and regularity. Economy of living, curiously enough, is marked by a spare use of ink. The terminals are abrupt and blunt, leaving off short. Where economy is the result of circumstances, not disposition, only some of the words are thus ended, while others have open, free curves, and the long letters are looped. Generosity and liberality may be seen likewise in the end curve of every word. Where these characteristics are inconstant and variable the disposition will be found to be uncertain—liberal in some matters, while needlessly economical and stingy in others.

A person fond of society writes the capital letter 'M' with the three upper curves on the same level. If the tail of this letter is carried far below the line, there is vulgarity of mind and imperfect education. Bars used instead of stops are the result of caution. The writer fears lest his sentences should be misinterpreted by being run into each other. When a bar is placed below the signature, it means tenacity of purpose, coupled with extreme caution; perhaps, also, a dread of criticism and adverse opinions. No dots to the letter 'i' means negligence, a want of attention to details, with but a small faculty of observation. When the dots are placed at random, neither above nor in proximity to the letter to which they belong, impressionability, want of reflection, and impulsiveness may be anticipated.

Ambition and gratified happiness give to the whole writing an upward tendency. Hopefulness lacks the firmness of ambition, and appears only in the signature which curves upwards, while the rest of the writing is impulsive, without much firmness.

Sorrow gives every line of the writing a downward inclination. Temporary affliction will at once show in the writing: a preoccupied mind, full of trouble, cares little whether the letter then written is legible or neat; hence the writing is erratic, uncertain, and the confusion of mind is clearly exhibited in every line. Irritable and touchy persons slope the flourishes only, such as the cross of the letter ' t ' and the upper parts of the capital letters. When the capital letters stand alone in front of the words, and the final letters also are isolated, it betokens great creative power and ideality, such as would form an author and clever writer.

The most personal part of a letter or document is, of course, the signature, but alone it is not a safe guide to character. The lines placed below or after it tell a great deal more than the actual name.

A curved bending line, ending in a hook, indicates coquetry, love of effect, and ideality.

An exaggerated, comma-like form of line means caprice, tempered by gravity of thought, and versatility of ideas.

An unyielding will—fiery, and at the same time determined—draws a firm hooked line after the name.

A wavy line shows great variety in mental power, with originality.

Resolution is shown by a plain line ; and extreme caution, with full power to calculate effect and reason a subject from every point of view, is shown by two lines and dots, thus ——:——.

To sum up the matter briefly, it will be observed that a clever person cares very little about the form of his writing—it is the matter alone which concerns him ; whereas, with a limited brain power, great care as to appearance is taken. But human nature is never a simple combination of elements, it is dependable upon a complexity of changes and chances.

It is said that with everyone a complete change takes place every seven years. Motives and circumstances all leave decided marks upon the character and mind of an individual. Not perhaps for years will innate virtues or vices become apparent, which have lain dormant, awaiting circumstances to develop them.

A collection of any person's old letters is very curious. Written from earliest childhood to extreme old age, a veritable life's history lies in the faded ink ; and to study character from handwriting fairly it can only be done from such authenticated examples.

Old letters written two or three hundred years ago are of great value for the purpose, because, so far as they are concerned, all party spirit and prejudice is dead, buried, and forgotten. Their biographers no longer fear the consequence of a too candid and personal account, and are therefore more likely to give a just and calm criticism of character, weighing evenly in the balance both virtues and vices. With historical characters it is curious to contrast the contemporary biographies with the graphologist's opinion of their handwriting, given without knowing whose the writing was.

Any collection of old MSS. is interesting, as showing the various styles of writing in vogue at different periods. Fashion or circumstances had some influence on this point. Royal marriages with foreign princesses brought England into contact with different nations. Wars in strange lands introduced alien words into our vocabulary, some of which speedily became naturalized, while others, voted slang, remained only for a short while and then disappeared. New words are constantly being coined, and take the place of others. This may seem a trivial matter, and irrelevant to the subject of old writing, but any points bearing on the subject must throw new light upon it and help to elucidate it.

The personality of a writer can never be wholly separated from his works. And in any question of date or authenticity of a document being

called in question, the value of graphology and
its theories will be found of the utmost importance; for the various changes in the style of
handwriting, or in the spelling of words, although
perhaps so minute and gradual as seldom to be
remarked, are, nevertheless, links in a chain which
it would be extremely hard to forge successfully
so as to deceive those acquainted with the matter
and well versed in its peculiarities.

CHAPTER III.

ANGLO-SAXON, NORMAN-FRENCH, LATIN, AND OLD ENGLISH.

ALTHOUGH we are always told that our present English language is directly derived from that of our Saxon forefathers, this information gives us very little, if any, help towards deciphering the old Anglo-Saxon documents. The Saxons, we are told, were not one nation, but rather composed of an aggregate of tribes of Germanic and Scandinavian origin, whose piratical instincts led them to seek adventure by sea and land and form new colonies, just as at the present day Englishmen go forth in search of fame and fortune in the uttermost parts of the earth.

Thus the Saxon language, although derived from one identical base, was a collection of dialects banded together, which, in its educated and scholastic form, greatly resembled German in its construction.

The language of the Anglo-Saxons (so far as
Great Britain is concerned) has been classified

EXTRACT FROM DOMESDAY.

under three distinct headings, the first being pure
Anglo-Saxon, *i.e.*, the language as spoken by the
first settlers, with an admixture of Celtic or

British ; secondly, this same combination with the addition of Danish ; and thirdly, the three above - named languages combined, with the further addition of Norman-French, having in all a Saxon dialect for the basis, to which were afterwards added new words brought into it by foreign invaders or emigrants from over the seas. Ever since the invention of printing great changes have taken place in our language, and to go back prior to that epoch reveals greater changes still.

The writings of early chroniclers and poets are so full of words and phrases now obsolete that many books and dictionaries have been compiled to explain their meanings.

The Lord's Prayer, as given in the Durham Book,* looks to us hopelessly foreign—only a few words are familiar.   The personal pronouns ' us,' ' we,' ' he,' ' him,' and the preposition ' to,' as well as the conjunction ' and,' are unchanged, but the verbs are conjugated quite differently to the correct English of to-day; still, if we would seek for a living example resembling old Saxon dialect, it can easily be found in several parts of England, such as Devonshire, Dorsetshire, and other counties, the country-folk still speaking almost

* This is a copy of the Gospels of the Anglo-Saxon period. It was formerly in the Cottonian Library, now in the Manuscript Department of the British Museum.   It is known as ' Nero D. iv.' Old Sir Robert Cotton had busts of the Roman Emperors over his book shelves, and the names survive.

pure Anglo-Saxon, though this is fast dying out
before the advance of education and Board school
science. The Anglo-Saxon alphabetical characters differ only from the Roman in the letter
'w,' written þ : there are also two additional
double letters—' th,' represented by the following
letter þ, and ' dh,' ð, these last being in frequent
use in the construction of words.

The early Saxon handwriting was bold and
clear. Most of it now existing consists of
monastic copies of books or charters. The
Saxons were a clever and industrious people,
plodding and practical. Their abbeys were more
of the nature of large seminaries or colleges, where
learning was carried on ; and in this respect the
northern parts of England were better supplied
than the south, a result caused probably by each
fresh influx of tribes landing on the northern
and eastern coasts of the country, and spreading
inland from thence. There seems to be no doubt
that the reign of King Alfred did much to promote
study and an increased attention to literature,
hitherto neglected except among a few professed
scholars.

A learned king would naturally set the fashion
to his subjects, and Alfred must have possessed
immense energy, for it was an extraordinary thing
for a middle - aged man to be able to educate
himself sufficiently to master the difficulties of a

foreign language so opposed in construction to
his own native tongue as Latin, which in nowise
resembles Saxon. He must have toiled hard to
have completed the many translations from Latin
into Saxon which are accredited to him.

Alfred was a popular hero, and, like all heroes,
was invested by tradition with the credit of every
improvement in literature or art which took place
within his era. Be this as it may, there is no
doubt that he did stimulate his fellow-countrymen
to make efforts towards self-improvement, by
setting them a practical example in himself.
Such examples are rare, unfortunately ; they
must always be productive of good results—an
' ounce of practice is worth a pound of precept.'

From the time of King Alfred's re-introduction
of Latin into this country it gradually gained
ground as the language of scholars. Learned
ecclesiastics coming to England found it convenient as the medium for exchange of thoughts
and ideas. It was for many centuries the accepted
' Volapuk,' understood by all who professed to
any learning.

Rome was the light of the western world, the
centre from whence religion and learning was
disseminated to the less enlightened parts of
Europe. Careful study of the old authors necessi-
tated an acquaintance with both Greek and
Latin. The emissaries of the Pope, either as

legates or missionaries, spread all over civilized Europe, and carried with them the learning of their age.

Intercourse between England and France was somewhat checked by dissensions and wars both at home and abroad, but with the Conquest came a large body of monks, for the chief wealth of Normandy was invested in its rich abbeys, from whence Duke William had borrowed large sums of money to fit out his expedition upon the security of his future possession of England. These loans he honestly and amply repaid by large grants of land out of his new kingdom ; hence new abbeys sprang up filled with foreign monks, who brought over their language, arts and sciences, to teach in the new country they had adopted as their own. The language of the court was of necessity Norman-French, which differs as much from the French of to-day as ancient from modern English. But a knowledge of French makes these early deeds easy to understand.

By degrees the Norman-French language came into use in legal matters, partially superseding Latin ; probably copies of deeds (rarely copies of the same deed are preserved) were made in both languages.

The lower orders of the people clung persistently to their own old Saxon tongue, a fact

NORMAN-FRENCH DEED.

clearly demonstrated by the way the old Saxon field-names are to the present day retained, and flowers, animals and matters of everyday country-life bear names of evident Saxon origin. The Saxons were a conquered race, and as such became the servants of their conquerors. The animals which in life they tended were eaten by the Norman nobles, who called them, when used as food, by names of French derivation. Thus the Saxon 'sheep' became 'mutton'; 'pig' turned into 'pork'; 'calf' into 'veal,' etc. With the names of many wild flowers French origin is traceable, especially with cultivated sorts. In Berkshire the village children call field-daisies ' margs,' abbreviated, without doubt, from the French *marguerite*. Among garden flowers there are pansies, French *pensé*; gillyflower, *girofle*, and many others; but as a whole there are few words of distinctly Latin origin to be found in the English language relating to every-day affairs. Norman-French did not come into immediate use in legal documents after the Conquest. The earliest deeds of the Norman kings were written in Latin, but after a while French superseded it for law work, but only for a comparatively short period, a statute being passed in the thirty-sixth year of King Edward III. deciding upon Latin as the law language of the realm, and from this date the use of Norman-French died out.

The growing dislike of the English to foreign prelates led to a steady resistance of their claims, culminating in the Statutes of Mortmain, Provisors and Præmunire, and finally in the suppression of all alien priories and foreign cells. This stopped the influx of French and Italian monks to our shores ; so it was that, after nearly four centuries, the Norman-French language died out and was forgotten. During the Middle Ages, and until the time of the Reformation, the monasteries still continued to be the principal seats of learning throughout the country, and Latin held its ground among scholars and lawyers. The introduction of printing, and finally the changes wrought by the Reformation, disturbed the pre-existing course of things. English gradually was settling down into its present form, and about the end of the fifteenth century it began to be used for law business transactions more and more. Latin, like Norman-French, had had its day and was dying out. Finally, by George III.'s Act of Parliament the native language was ordered to be used for law work, and now Latin has become obsolete, so far as practical work is concerned ; and understanding old legal Latin— once a necessity for a lawyer—has now become an antiquarian profession. One relic of Anglo-Saxon remained on in our language for many centuries. The double letter þ, 'th,' will be found in the written copies of monkish chartularies for place-names beginning with 'th.' Even so late as the fifteenth century we find it freely employed in English documents. I possess a copy of the criminal charges made against De la Pole, Duke of Suffolk, for high treason, 1450.* Throughout the manuscript the Saxon þ appears in such words as ' other,' 'that,' ' the,' etc., which look curious written ' oþer,' ' þᵗ,' ' þe.'

About the time when printing was brought over and practised in England the Saxon þ disappeared. The þ in some words was printed ' y,' which continued in use until the present century. I am not aware of any place-names having been altered by this change of lettering, but it is quite possible that some changes may have occurred through it. It would be easy for a person unaccustomed to the Saxon þ to mistake it for other letters ; nor would it sound phonetically wrong, as either ' th,' ' p,' or 'y' must be followed either by a vowel or the consonant 'r,' 'ph' in old documents being usually replaced by an 'f.'

Of late years many absurd mistakes have been made by Ordnance Surveyors who, mistaking the local dialect or from preconceived ideas as to what the names ought to be, have set down many incorrectly. On this subject I wrote recently in a paper in the *Berkshire Archæological*

* Now in the Bodleian Library at Oxford.

Magazine. A man from the South of England fails to comprehend the northern or western dialects. Country-folk from the north cannot understand a word spoken by southerners; this also would account for errors. Spelling of course has altered; it is no safe guide towards derivation; phonetic pronunciation of a word is more likely to give a clue to the origin. Field-names have been handed down orally from generation to generation; and it is very curious to observe how faithfully the phonetic sounds have been preserved among an illiterate people, long after the meanings of the words have disappeared.

The Saxons named their fields from ordinary things, or surroundings, or the animals who fed in the meadows. The following Saxon words may be found occurring constantly as field-names:

Æcne, fruitful; *Æcer,* field; *Æbesn* or *Æfesne,* pasture; *Ata, Atih,* tares, or oats, the latter were common.

Birce, birch-tree.

Cyrc, Cyrce, Cyrice, Circ, Circe, church, the last two most common; *Culfre,* a dove; *Cealc,* chalk; *Ceorl,* churl or husbandman.

Ent, a giant; *Eorisc,* a bulrush: *Errich,* stubble; *Enid* or *Ened* a duck; *Emn,* even.

Fearras, Ferris, oxen.

Fearh, a little pig ; *Fearh-Cwæl,* swine-fever.

Getreminc, fortress ; *Gat* or *Yat,* a goat.

Halga, a saint ; *halig,* holy ; *Hyd,* a hide ; *Ham,*
home, homestead ; *Hurst,* or *Hyrst,* a wood ;
Holt, a grove ; *Hleotan,* to cast lots (meadows
were held in lots, or allotments, from a very
early period, and so continued up to the time
of the Enclosure Acts) ; *Hluton,* part allotted ;
Halm, stubble.

Ith yrnth, arable ; *Ilt,* a sow.

Ley, Lea, Leaze or *Lay, Lye,* meadow or grass-
land.

Neolnes, more properly spelt *Neowlnes,* an abyss.

On-æl, a burning.

Rene, a course ; *Riip,* harvest.

Sul, a plough ; *Stret,* or *Stræt,* a street or public
highway.

Wong, a meadow ; *Welig,* a willow ; *Wegleast,* a
going out of the way ; *Wer,* an enclosure.

The law-Latin, as used in England, degenerated
greatly ; it became interspersed with words of
native origin, Latinized by the lawyer. Old
court-rolls especially are full of obsolete words ;
so too are the public rolls, but there are now
many dictionaries explaining their meanings,
although, of course, here and there an unknown
word may occur, yet the context will usually explain or help towards its significance. As a

whole, the English language has changed more during the present century than at any time of the preceding ages. Railway and telegraph have brought all parts of the kingdom into closer contact, and also with foreign countries, which would account for constant alterations in language and customs.

The legal Latin became, finally, merely a series of mechanical forms; these at last were translated into English. For this reason a careful study of the wording of a deed of the eighteenth century in English will show that it is the counterpart of the same class of document in its older Latin form.

CHAPTER IV.

OLD DEEDS.

AMONG old family papers it is rare to meet with many dating further back than the Reformation; first of all, this may be accounted for by the enormous amount of land possessed by the monks, who, instead of having to search through deeds, entered these grants and gifts of property into their charter-book. The monastic estates, after the Dissolution, were managed through the Augmentation Office; many of the original deeds were destroyed or lost in the general confusion, and a new distribution of the lands took place by the king irrespective of the former owners, whose claims were totally ignored, although in such grants or deeds of gift the name of the monastery formerly owning the property is usually named.

The king must have realized large sums of money by these transactions, which were carried out through his commissioners or agents, and not usually granted direct from the Crown; very little of the land confiscated from the abbeys was retained as royal property, but appears to have been almost immediately sold or granted away.

But to begin from the oldest reliable period at which deeds may refer to, is to go back to the Norman Conquest, or rather, to the time when the lands had been distributed among the Norman noblemen, as described in the famous Domesday Book, compiled it is said between 1080 and 1085. Reference is therein made to previous Saxon possessors; but only in very few instances can any certain information be obtained of private property prior to the eleventh century.

Private deeds do exist between the time of William I. and Richard I.; from this latter king's reign, about A.D. 1179, legal memory dates; but usually the earliest family deeds are of Edward I., because then it was that the legal era was fixed to commence. This king has been, so far as regards manorial rights and customs, rightly called the 'English Solon.' He passed innumerable Acts of Parliament on the subject of legal matters; he revised the whole of the national laws, retaining but improving existing arrangements. A most interesting account of early English law and manorial customs is published by the Selden Society. It is very rare indeed to discover private deeds earlier than this ; but, of course, every rule has its exception.

To prove a title to property it is now only requisite to show a twenty years' possession of it. Papers forming the title deeds to farms or small holdings are seldom of any great age. The custom of depositing estate records in the care of the family lawyer has tended to preserve a few deeds; but, on the other hand, has resulted in much wholesale destruction of useless but curious documentary evidence.

Parchment being an animal substance (usually made from the skin of sheep), if kept in a damp place, soon begins to decay and become offensive, mites readily attack it, dirt and dust accumulate rapidly on its external woolly surface—all these make a search among hoards of old deeds anything but a pleasant or a cleanly occupation.

The usual storehouse for such collections was some unused garret or stable-loft, where rats and mice ran riot and birds flew in and out as they liked. Forgotten, perhaps, for several generations, the old papers lay untouched till death or removal brought changes, and the deeds were either placed in safer keeping, or else—alas! the most usual course—were consigned to the flames as useless rubbish.

Even now lawyers find great difficulty in preserving and storing the deeds entrusted to their

charge. The dangers of fire and damp are con-
flicting, and to avoid the one may bring about
greater risk from the other cause. Vast numbers
of deeds have been sold when a lawyer's office
has been broken up. These papers, having lain
for years unclaimed until the ownership was lost
or forgotten, finally were sold to some antiquarian bookseller or antiquary, or else the skin
was cleansed and used again; parchment being
a valuable substance. It is employed in many
trades. From it size is prepared. Gold-beaters
employ it largely, and also to the bookbinders'
trade it is essential, besides having many other
and varied uses.

The quality of parchment varies much. That
upon which early deeds, those about the thirteenth
century, are written, is in small pieces, woolly in
texture and of a dark brown shade. In the sixteenth century the sheets are larger, smoother,
and yellow, becoming whiter in colour and more
even as its preparation was better understood and
practised.

Vellum was a finer sort of parchment prepared
from the skins of very young or still-born animals.
Of it the old manuscript books were made,
adorned with illuminations and miniature paintings, which required a fine, smooth surface, and
vellum was free from the flaws which frequently
occur in the skins of mature animals.

With the history of paper-making we have nothing to do. Paper was known as early as the thirteenth century, but for law work in England it was seldom, if ever, employed before the fourteenth century. The earliest known examples are described as being made of silk manufactured abroad, where it was used for illuminated work in place of vellum—at least, so Prou states, but does not tell us of any notable examples.

The history of English-made paper is somewhat obscure. Ordinary books published for the enlightenment of the young state that the first English paper-mill was erected at Dartford, in Kent, by Speilman, a German, in 1588. This, however, must be wrong, for in that popular educator of the past generation, the *Saturday Magazine*, a short account is given of early paper and its water-marks, and John Tate is named as having a mill at Hertford, his device being a star of five points enclosed within a double circle. John Tate the younger is here stated to have made the paper for the first book printed on English-made paper about the year 1496. It was written in Latin, and entitled 'Bartholomeus de Proprietatibus Rerum.' His mark upon it was a wheel. This same account goes on to say that the paper used by the early printers bore great variety of marks—the ox-head, with the star between the horns; the black letter ⅌; the shears; an open hand, surmounted

by a star; a collared dog's head, with a trefoil
above it; a crown, an orb, a shield charged with
a bend, and many other devices. Hone, in his
'Everyday Book,' also gives a few other marks.
He mentions the orb as a foreign paper-mark
existing as early as 1301, and says it is the
'oldest known mark.'

Hand-paper is the kind usually found used for
early documents. It was a convenient size for
court-rolls or legal writings. The name arose
from its water-mark, that of an open hand with a
star above the middle finger. This is found both
in England and Germany. Its date of manufacture was certainly older than 1450. The actual
device varied. Sometimes the fingers were raised
in blessing, sometimes it was a hand encased in
a glove or gauntlet. The star had sometimes five
and at others six points.

On some coarse whitish-brown paper of 1465 a
garter was used; about the same date a bull or
bull's head appears. These were detached sheets,
but probably there was no distinction then
between book or letter paper.

A careful study of paper-marks would be interesting and valuable if the authenticity or age
of old papers were doubted, though the question
of forgery scarcely ever arises, for so much knowledge and ingenuity would be required to produce
a manuscript which would deceive an adept and

pass muster as a veritable antique, that fraud of this kind is well-nigh impossible.

Paper was not known in France, and consequently not used, before 1130. It did not reach as far north as Normandy until the fourteenth century; therefore it is improbable that it found its way into England till after this date, or, if so, only in very small quantities. The oldest paper is coarse and rough, scarcely sized at all, so that the ink sank into it like blotting-paper, making erasures impossible.

Supposing even that paper was made in England in the fifteenth and sixteenth centuries, the quantities produced here were very small and inadequate to meet the demand; hence the chief supply was of foreign manufacture even until a comparatively recent period.

The Netherlands and Germany were the great paper-producing countries. It was a state privilege, and the water-marks used were either the arms of the royal patron or a crest or badge of the manufacturer, so by this means the precise locality of some of these ancient manufacturers may be ascertained.

The history of old paper-marks sadly needs a Chaffers or a Cripps to investigate the matter. No such collection has ever been attempted, nor has the subject hitherto met with the attention it demands and deserves. Perhaps, now that antiquarianism is becoming so fashionable, this, like other kindred sciences, will find some followers.

Another important part of a deed is the ink with which it was written. Each scribe had his own particular receipt for making it, the principal ingredients being oak galls and sulphate of iron. Many chemicals are recommended as restoratives for faded ink, but these should be avoided as far as possible, as they are liable to stain and disfigure the parchment, and in the end make matters worse. Familiarity with particular handwritings after some practice will enable the reader to make out otherwise unintelligible words without any other assistant than a powerful magnifying glass.

If the ink is very faint the simplest and most harmless restorative is sulphate of ammonia; but its loathsome smell once endured is not easily forgotten; the experiment in consequence is very seldom repeated, for the result is scarcely good enough to risk a repetition of so horrible a smell.

Coloured inks or pigments were seldom, if ever, employed for legal documents. The use of these was restricted to the cloister, requiring manipulation by an illuminator instead of a mere scribe. Red, blue and green were in use; these were mineral colours. The red was composed either of red lead or oxide of iron, the green from copper, and the blue from lapis lazuli finely powdered, or else it, too, like the green, was prepared from an oxide of copper.

Illuminating was a separate profession apart from that of writing. The charter or missal was finished by the scribe, and then handed over to the artist to be adorned with fanciful capital letters and elaborate scroll-works. Such ornamentation was unnecessary for legal documents, yet sometimes these had fancy headings, which, like the illuminations, were put in after the writing was finished, as is proved by the occasional omission of them, although space is left where they ought to have been filled in.

Seals and sealing-wax deserve a few words. These came into use gradually. The earliest deeds are very small, and have very small insignificant seals.

It is said that neither the Saxon or Norman noblemen could sign their own names, but instead employed the Christian sign of the cross (still in use among the illiterate) as their pledge of good faith, and to witness their consent and approval. The Normans perhaps introduced the use of seals as appendices to deeds as a further proof that the deed itself was approved and executed. A man's seal or signet was always regarded as his most sacred possession. It was destroyed after death to avoid its being used for fraudulent purposes.

The use of signet-rings is very ancient. Many

old Saxon and Roman signets have been dug up
from time to time in various parts of England;
but small private seals bearing devices do not
appear to have been attached to deeds earlier
than the fourteenth and fifteenth centuries.

Many of the large wax seals are very beautiful,
but few, alas! exist in any state of perfection.
The wax used for them was either its natural
colour or else a sealing-wax of a very dark green,
almost black, or red; white, also, was used, now
discoloured by age into a dingy yellow. Yellow
wax was also common. Besides the royal seals,
each abbey had its own particular seal, upon which
was either a view of the abbey, a portrait of its
patron saint, or its badge or shield. Many of these
are described by Dugdale in the 'Monasticon,'
but he was unable to discover the devices pertaining to the lesser houses or cells. The fashion for
seals died out, till at last only royal grants or
similar documents of the sixteenth century have
them attached. In the Georgian period we find
small private seals placed on the margin of
deeds. These were not always the arms and
crest of the person against whose signature they
appear, but perhaps belonged to the lawyer or
one of the contracting parties. Here it is that a
knowledge of heraldry is extremely useful.

The size and shape of a deed at first glance
goes far with the experienced reader to determine

its age, even before a single word of it has been read ; likewise the general aspect will give a slight hint as to the possible contents without deciphering any of it.

The deeds relative to the earliest grants of land are very small, a marked contrast to the voluminous sheets of parchment considered necessary to a modern conveyance or deed. The writing often was minute, but each letter was carefully formed. Many early deeds are in far better preservation than some of those written several centuries later, when less attention was paid to the materials on which they were indited, or the ink used.

CHAPTER V.

LAW TECHNICALITIES.

THE two chief divisions into which all law deeds may be roughly classified are the deed-poll and the indenture. The former is a square piece of parchment, made by one person, such as a will or a bond ; while the indenture was the work of several parties. Of this latter kind are deeds of trusteeship, marriage settlements, mortgages, and sales or transfers of land.

The indenture was so called from the fact that its upper edge was vandyked, or indented—a very secure but primitive method of testing authenticity ; each party had a copy. These duplicates were written on a single strip of parchment merely cut asunder afterwards, through a word written between the two copies, such as 'chirographum,' so that when required to be produced as evidence the two divided portions and words would fit each other exactly—indisputable evidence of their originality, both simple and ingenious.

A very common form of deed, met with among title-deeds, is the 'Fine,' technically so-called from its opening sentence : 'Hic est finalis concordia facta in curia Domini Regis'; the sovereign's name follows with the year of accession, after which are the names of the buyer and seller of the property, a full description of the amount of acreage, tenements, etc. After warranting the whole for life to its purchaser, the deed concludes with the sum of money paid for the property; this is written in words, not figures. These deeds are more puzzling to amateurs than any other. The 'Fines' are narrow strips of parchment, two in number; they are closely covered with black lettering, making them at first difficult to decipher.

This transfer of land by 'fine' originated at first from an actual suit at law commenced to recover possession of the lands, and by this means to establish a clear indisputable title to it; in course of time the suit was discontinued, but the form of wording was retained by custom.

'A "fine,"' says Blackstone, 'is so called because it puts an end to the suit (from the Latin word *finis*, an end), which, when once decided, puts an end not only to that suit, but also to all other controversies concerning the same matter, for by this means an absolute sale was effected,

𝔉orm of 𝔉ine.

1.—Hæc est finalis Concordia facta in Curia Domini Regis apud . . . in . . . anno regni Regis . . .

2.—Coram . . . . et aliis fidelibus domini Regis tunc ibi præsentibus . . .

3.—Inter A B, petentem, et C D, tenentem [per E F, positum loco ipsius C D, ad lucrandum vel perdendum] . . .

4.—De . . . . } In terra, in prata, in pascuis, in molendinis, in stagnis, et in omnibus pertinentiis ejusdem terræ.

5.—Unde placitum fuit inter eos in Curia domini Regis, scilicet	Unde recognitio de morte antecessoris summonita fuit inter eos in præfata Curia, viz.,
6.—Quod idem[1] C D, concessit eidem A B, et heredibus suis totam terram, etc. [The appurtenances are here sometimes set out at length.]	Quod idem[1] C D, quietum clamavit pro se et heredibus suis totum jus et clamium qd. habuit in tota terra, etc.	Quod idem[1] C D, recognovit totam terram, etc., esse jus et hereditatem ipsius A B [ut illa quæ idem A B, habuit de dono prædicti C D] et terram illam quietam clamavit a se et heredibus suis imperpetuum.
7.—Prædicto A B, et heredibus suis imperpetuum.	Et assignatis suis præterquam viris religiosis.

8.—Et pro hac

9.—Concessione	recognitione	remissione	quieta clamantia	fine et concordia.

10.—Prædictus A B.

[1] Idem, *or* prædictus, *or* præfatus, *or* memoratus.

11.—Dedit predicto C D.			

. . solidos esterling . . marcas argenti . . besantia . . denarios.　　unam juvencam ... unum ostorium sorum

Concessit prædictæ terræ A B, totam vestituram predictæ terræ pro anno.

Quietum clamavit imperpetuum totam terram quam tenuit de illo in X. prædicto et heredibus suis C D.

Concessit predicto C D et heredibus suis . . . acras prædictæ terræ scil . . [*or* totam prædictam terram] (in subinfeudation as then mentioned).

12.—Et prædictus C D, et heredes ejus warantizabunt eidem A B, prædicta tenementa, etc., cum pertinentiis contra omnes homines [qui de stirpe suo exierint.]

[Here the fine, especially if it is of early date, will end; but in cases of subinfeudation, where rent or services are reserved, the following forms occur after 6.]

13.—Habend[a] et tenend[a] eidem A B, de prædicto C D, et heredibus suis imperpetuum (*or* tota vita sua).

14.—Reddendo inde per ann. (tota vita ipsius) . . . . . *s.* ad terminos scilicet medietatem ad festum S^{ci} . . . . et aliam [alteram] ad festum S^{ci} . . . . pro omnibus serviciis consuetudinibus et exactionibus ad prædictum C D, et heredes ejus pertinentibus.

15.—Et faciendo inde Capitalibus dominis de feodo (*or*, feodi illius) pro prædicto C D, omnia alia servicia quæ ad illa tenementa, etc., pertinent [salvo forinseco servitio].

16.—If the grant was for the tenant's life only, this occurs :—Et post decessum ipsius A B, prædicta tenementa cum pertinenciis integre revertentur ad prædictum C D, quieta de heredibus ipsius A B, tenenda de capitalibus dominis feodi illius per servitia quæ ad illa pertinent.

17.—If the rent was reserved during the grantor's life only, then this :—Et post decessum ipsius C D, prædictus A B, et heredes ejus erunt quieti de solutione prædicti redditus imperpetuum.

18.—If the fine is to entail the property the habendum clause will run thus :—Habendum et tenendum { eisdem A B, et E F, eidem A B, et heredibus { et hered . . de corporibus eorum inter eos procreatis. { quos idem A B, de corpore E F, uxoris ejus [legitime] procreaverit.

and all previous claims upon the property were made void.'

Sale by fine is of very ancient date. Instances of it are said to be known prior to the Norman invasion. We may, therefore, conclude that it was probably an old Saxon custom, or was devised in later times as a certain means to avoid dispute and disagreement arising from an imperfect title of possession.

There are several legal varieties of 'fines,' but these are of little consequence to the antiquary, whose interest lies only in the names, dates, and localities mentioned, and, so long as the land changed its ownership, cares little about the technical process by which the transfer was made.

Another way of making a good title so as to legalize and effect a complete sale of property was that known as "Sale by Recovery.' This also consisted of a law-suit, at first real, then imaginary.

The prescribed form was very complicated. Explanations of it are to be found in most books on law subjects, but the matter lies in a nutshell. One man desired to sell certain land which another man was anxious to purchase; whereupon the would-be purchaser issued a writ, in which he pretended to claim the land; at this stage of the affair a third party, not really concerned in any way in it, was brought forward to warrant the title of the real owner, who then

20716
Pro ꝑ̃ et terris in Com.
Nottingham̄ · 1

FORM OF FINE.

came forward bringing a witness proving ownership to his property; thus an undisputable title
to the land was established. A deed of recovery
is then issued, rehearsing the whole transaction,
agreeing that a certain sum of money, equivalent
to the value of the land, should be paid by the
purchaser; and here the bargain was concluded,
and the curtain fell on the legal farce.

Some of these recovery deeds are quite works
of art. They are written in courthand, on large
squares of parchment, smooth and white. The
heading and capital letter are ornamented with
scroll-work in pen and ink. Generally an en-
graved portrait of the reigning sovereign was
added. Part of this ornamentation was done by
hand and the rest completed with steel engraving.
The most elaborate deeds are those of the Stuart
monarchs, especially towards the end of the
seventeenth century, but after the time of the
second George these well-executed deeds dis-
appear.

The oldest statute relating to Recoveries of
which I find any mention is of the commencement of the reign of Henry VII., but I have not
met with any as early in date as this.

A beginner finds much difficulty in deciding
between deeds of sale or appointment of trustees
for the safe custody of land to secure marriage
portions and deeds of mortgage; all these three

deeds are, in point of size and general outline, nearly identical; the experienced lawyer can detect them at once ; he needs only to study what is called the operative part of the document, avoiding any waste of time which wading through the technical phrases involves.

One of the commonest forms of deeds met with relative to the sale of land are those known as 'Lease and Release,' a method invented by Sergeant Moore in the reign of Henry VIII., which, from its simplicity, speedily became very popular, and superseded the other forms of sale.

The principal deeds referring to a Lease and Release are two in number. The smaller of these is generally found wrapped up within the larger parchment, as the two had to be kept together, being in reality part and parcel of each other. The smaller parchment was the lease drawn up between the parties; by it a formal lease for a year of the premises or land was granted by the owner to the purchaser, but no mention of any rent or sum of money is made in it, and herein is the difference between the sale-lease and an ordinary lease, for in this latter both the term of years and the yearly rental are expressly named.

The ' Release,' or larger parchment, is dated a day following the lease which it cancels, hereby gaining its name of ' release.' It is in reality the actual deed of sale, for the price paid for the land will be found in it, and a full and complete warranty securing it for ever to the purchaser.

An ordinary lease of premises is worded similarly to the above, but differs from it in several ways; usually it is a larger sheet of parchment. The term of years varies from three, five, seven, to twenty-one, at a fixed rent paid either half-yearly or quarterly at the four principal feasts, Lady Day, or the Feast of the Annunciation, the Feast of St. John, or Midsummer, St. Michael and All Angels, better known as Michaelmas, and the Feast of the Nativity, popularly called Christmas Day. These deeds commence with the date of the day, month and year, followed by the names of the persons contracting the agreement, with those of their co-trustees, or witnesses, usually selected from among relatives or connections by marriage, or else immediate neighbours. An exact terrier of the land is given, its locality, field-names, and acreage. Three parts of the way down the sheet of parchment will be found the rent and term of years for which the land is granted, together with stipulations as to repairs, rights of ingress and egress; any services, customs or heriots, whether due in kind or by payment; last of all comes the warrant against intruders. Of course, with deeds of sale there are other legal documentary forms, with variations of wording, but the two last above described are those generally met with.

The oldest form of sale is called a 'feoffment' or grant. Externally it differs little in appearance from a 'fine,' at least as regards its earliest form, both being very small closely-written deeds; the first was in the set lawyer type of handwriting, while a 'fine' was indited in courthand.

A 'feoffment,' or grant, was the oldest and simplest form of document; but in later times it was followed by a deed 'of Uses' which required many other deeds to follow in its wake before a permanent and satisfactory sale was effected.

It is all these legal formalities which make the reading of old deeds so unnecessarily confusing; their intricacies can only be mastered by careful study of books on legal matters, and a comparison of the several kinds of deeds above enumerated. A mortgage deed differs from the sales or leases in several particulars; firstly, the term of years granted is usually absurdly long, nine hundred or a thousand years, perhaps; while in lieu of money, the nominal rent of one peppercorn yearly, or some equally insignificant equivalent was demanded. In place of the rent in an ordinary lease, the real reason of the mortgage is given in full, with the date and appointed place where and when the borrowed money is to be repaid. Often the vicarage, or the parson's house, was chosen—perhaps considered as an additional guard against fraud,

and that the clergyman as a witness, being a
disinterested party, would see justice done on
both sides. No mortgage deeds are old; the
older ones, if they existed, were probably destroyed
as soon as the transaction was finished. Most
of those found among family papers are of the
eighteenth and nineteenth centuries, and refer to
small pieces of land or cottages, showing that
even then the small owners became involved in
debts and difficulties, being obliged to raise
money upon their holdings until finally the land
itself had to be sold to satisfy the demands of the
creditors, the purchaser usually being the nearest
large landed proprietor, who paid a better price
for what would join on to and complete the area
of his estate. These small holdings had probably
been accumulated bit by bit out of the waste.
First, perhaps, the settler rigged up a primitive
dwelling, or hut; the old tradition being that if
a roofed dwelling could be erected in one night
a claim to the land was thereby established. If
undisturbed, the squatter would gradually extend
his boundaries; but a small rent was generally
demanded by the lord of the manor as an ac-
knowledgment of the encroachment; these little
holdings are called 'key-holdings,' and are to be
found in all parts of England.

At present there is a growing desire to increase
the number of small proprietors; 'fashion,' it is

said, 'repeats itself periodically.' Former experience showed the result of small holders to be a failure; no land, however small in acreage, can be worked without capital; a succession of bad seasons cause immediate loss and continuous outlay without a compensating return ; debts once begun, are apt to accumulate ; all trades are worked cheaper on a wholesale scale. Bit by bit, as failure comes, the small pieces of land will roll up into large properties again, like balls of quicksilver separated only for awhile.

Many of the deeds of mortgage are sad and silent witnesses of the gradual decay and downfall of old families.

The squire raised money to pay off trusts, legacies, and dowers. He pledged his mansion ; and in the inventory of his household effects we can study many queer facts. Our ancestors' homes were scantily furnished ; such lists surprise us, for they show what a very small amount of furniture was formerly considered necessary to render a house habitable.

Among family papers there is often another class of deeds altogether : one is a small square piece of parchment, with a huge seal attached ; this is often enclosed in a rough tin case or box. These are advowson deeds, or presentation of Church preferment. The gifts of many Church livings are in private hands. It was originally an hereditary property, and there are cases of it of very great antiquity ; but private family deeds referring to church property are seldom found earlier than the Jacobean period, and very seldom as old as that.

The earliest presentations or appointments to parochial duty were no doubt purely ecclesiastical, but with the Norman accession the secular and ecclesiastical affairs merged into closer proximity; it was considered a religious privilege to rebuild or erect a church. This the lord of the manor generally undertook, or perhaps originally as a private chapel or chantry. The appointment of an officiating priest became an ecclesiastical matter, being often granted to the monasteries by the patrons. To avoid the encroachment of lay interference, Thomas à Beckett first ordered that no clergyman should be instituted to a living without a bishop's approval and permission ; but there were often disputes on this subject. Few neighbourhoods existed without a monastery somewhere in the locality, and from the nearest religious house a candidate was probably selected ; finally, the right of presentation was claimed by the monastery, with whom it may have, by custom or by deed of gift, previously rested. Some education and a knowledge of Latin was essential for a priest, and education was almost entirely confined to the monks or their pupils. Thomas à Beckett, as archbishop, issued his mandate on the subject of parochial presentations as a means of retaining such institutions in episcopal hands, and so avoiding any appeals to the Pope which might be made by his legates or the abbots. With the monasteries, the chantries also passed away, soon being forgotten; numberless small unbeneficed chapels were then allowed to fall into ruins; the sites even of these now having been lost.

Deeds recounting the appointment of chantry priests are rare, and always possess some points of interest; often chantry priests were appointed by bequest, and sums of money left for their maintenance. These appear, however, to have been entirely distinct from the parish priest, although perhaps the office may eventually have merged into one and the same.

There seems from earliest times to have existed a jealousy between Cathedral bodies and the monks; but as the monastic orders waxed more and more wealthy and influential, we lose sight of the contention, and on all questions of early Church history there yet needs an impartial writer to decide many matters which at present are still uncertain, and are viewed by different writers according to their own particular religious bias, whether Anglican or Roman; hence, as history, they are too prejudiced to be entirely relied upon.

A sheriff formerly was the most important

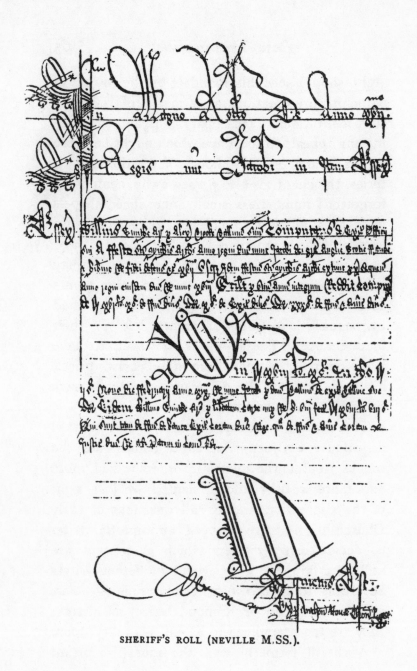

SHERIFF'S ROLL (NEVILLE M.SS.).

personage in his county, being the ambassador or representative of the sovereign. He was appointed directly by the Crown; even at the present day the names of three county gentlemen are written down and supposed to be presented to the Queen, who pricks the name of the man chosen to be sheriff; but really the names follow in sequence, each out-going sheriff adding a fresh name to the list previous to his own being erased as having served his turn.

The formal deed of appointment as sheriff was a narrow parchment strip, with a fine seal attached to it; his discharge from office was a very unimportant-looking document.

The sheriff's roll was the yearly bill of expenses incurred in the king's name by his sheriff or representative; as a rule they are not very interesting, although here and there the names of men appointed to local offices may appear, facts which might interest the local historian; but he would have to wade through the contents of many rolls before he extracted any information worth his attention, and much time would have to be expended over such a search. These rolls are long broad strips of parchment stitched together; the upper edge is sometimes cut square, and at others cut into a point or peak.

The wording runs as follows:

'In Magno Rotulo de anno . . . Regis . . . in Comitatu.'

A list of the sheriffs of England (Henry I. to fourth year of Edward III.) is to be found in the thirty-first report, page 262, of the deputy keeper of the Public Records. In some counties, sheriff-lists with additional genealogies and notes have been compiled, giving a very good county history of the oldest families of the shire.

A royal pardon was a deed-poll with a beautiful seal attached to it. It commenced with the sovereign's name. The writing was exact and well executed. The deed was divided into clauses or sections, the commencing word of each being written in very clear black letter. After the word 'Sciatis' comes the royal license and the name of its recipient, who is forgiven 'all rebellion and insurrection against the Crown, all homicide, felony, robbery or participation with such,' and the pardoned subject is permitted to retain his possessions; the word 'Perdonamus' coming about the centre of the document.

Unfortunately no information is given in the Charter in any way as to the particular cause for pardon being granted or the offence committed. This can only be guessed at by the help of English history, and a probable reason be assigned from among the many disputed accessions, civil wars, religious controversies of bygone centuries, all probable sources of high treason against the Crown.

Few old families were exempt from charges of treason, if they chanced to take any part in public affairs or were known to have been stanch adherents to prohibited religion.

A bond is a small paper or parchment—on one side written in English, on the other in Latin—the promise to repay or pay money due; generally the bond is in Latin, and the conditions of it written in English. Bonds were made out on the sale of property, or for mortgages or legacies : they occur in numbers among family papers.

These are the principal kinds of deeds met with, being the commonest legal forms. If others are found of an unusual character they should be put aside for closer investigation when practice has given greater experience, or be submitted to an expert for examination.

CHAPTER VI.

MANOR AND COURT ROLLS.

THE oldest account of an estate is to be obtained, not from deeds of purchase and mortgage, but from its own private records, called court rolls, a most curious class of documents, puzzling to the antiquary because they contain local words obsolete and not recognisable through derivation. Manor rolls are a study in themselves, a subject hitherto overlooked. They give us an insight into the most primitive form of local government, showing the manner in which lawlessness and disregard of laws were kept under, before a regular magisterial jurisdiction came into existence. The local manor court occupied the position and did the work now undertaken by the magistrates, County Court judges, and County Councils. When complaints are raised as to an excessive imposition of fines for trivial misdemeanours by any of these modern means of justice, I would advise the com-

plainants to study some old court rolls, wherein
may be read, ' Fines imposed for offences no longer
punishable.' The villager was fined if he kept
dogs or pigeons, for trespass in the woods, stealing
brushwood, for illegal fishing, for fighting, for
allowing animals to stray and become impounded.
Nor, unless he was a freedman, was he allowed to
marry or give in marriage without his lord's permission. All this sounds very arbitrary and
severe; in reality it probably was not so. The
bond between landlord and tenant must have been
a very close one. They were drawn into near
connection one with another; the well-being of
one meant the welfare of the other. Nor was the
meting forth of justice left solely in the hands of
the lord of the manor, but rather to the twelve
jurymen who formed the court itself. Certainly,
this self-government opened a means for unfair
influence and revenge of petty quarrels. This
was guarded against as far as possible. A very
common item brought before the court was the
accusation of wrongful information laid by a man
against his neighbour in direct opposition to the
ninth commandment.

There were two sections of manor courts—the
Court Leet and the Court Baron. The former
dealt with offences committed by the tenantry, and
contained much that is entertaining and curious;
the other was occupied with the tenants and their

holdings, of which they had every year to give account to the lord of the manor. Upon the death of a tenant, or the expiration of the lease, new presentments were made to the landlord for admission to the premises, or a fresh life added to the lease from time to time. In these rolls we find notices of heriots and other old services due from the tenants of certain lands; indeed, these old customs are not yet wholly extinct, though they have frequently fallen into abeyance. On some estates, heriots are still due, but, as a rule, have for many generations been compounded for by a money payment, just in the same way that feudal service passed into small sums of money and finally died out, or eventually took the form of money rent.

On many farms it was part of the rent to give the landlord yearly geese or cheese. In a small farm of ours in Cheshire the tenant had to give a cheese yearly, cart coals, keep a dog and a fighting cock for his landlord. All these dues are now gradually being given up.

The manorial history of England would carry us back very far did we attempt to trace it to its earliest beginnings. Perhaps the very first step towards it was the settlement of the Saxon tribes, who, in appropriating and distributing the land, laid the foundation of hereditary ownership. There is no rule or limit as to how many manors there might be in each parish. Clearly the parish was the older division of the two; nor can the creation of a manor be dated in any way, for many of the old manors were subsequently split up into two or more lesser ones. The affixes or manorial names are known to have, in some instances, varied with the family who held the land. Almost without exception, these manorial names were directly derived from the possessors. Few are older than the Norman period, perhaps having supplanted those in existence previously. Where double parochial names are used, the first is usually Saxon, the affix being a Norman addition, showing the fusion of the two races, which, though living in close proximity, were yet totally distinct from each other.

During the Middle Ages, manors were further subdivided, easily to be accounted for in this way: The owner of a manor was at first start the tenant of some wealthy and powerful nobleman, who, owning vast tracts of land, sub-let it out in manors, which were after some generations bought outright, or looked upon almost as freehold. The tenant was the resident squire of the place, living on the land, and farming it with the assistance of his children and dependents. After a time the family grew up, the sons married and needed homes of their own. In those days no one moved far away from the birthplace. What was more natural than that the squire should provide homes for his children close around the old manor-house, and, dividing off the property by the manorial boundaries, give to each a portion for self-maintenance ?   This accounts for the large, old-fashioned farmhouses to be found in most country parishes. The history of each farm, if investigated, will furnish a curious proof of the conservatism with which certain boundaries were preserved, and the manors regarded as sections seldom subdivided except into recognised lesser manors.

Society was very primitive two or three hundred years ago. It was then possible to live comfortably and make a living out of the land. No foreign grain was imported to affect the prices of corn in country places. Competition was unknown, and the people led a quiet, uneventful existence, following in the footsteps of their fore-fathers. Gradually changes have come about. The old race of yeomen have died out ; the few that are left make us forcibly regret that this should be the case.

The yeoman was a man of good education and long pedigree ; he belonged to the largest section of English society, called ' middle class.' Agriculture was his profession ; he seldom left home, consequently had few opportunities of spending money ; the character and personal history of every human being on the place was intimately known to him, for the villagers lived and died in their native villages. The roads were bad, therefore traffic from place to place was restricted to what was absolutely necessary. Posts and passenger coaches were rarities, and when first started met with little patronage from the majority of the people.

To return to the manorial courts. These were held but once during the year. It was the annual audit of the freemen on the estate, the 'Visus franciplegii,' as the opening words of the court roll states.

Quarter sessions were held four times in the year, while the sheriff's tourn took place half yearly. These inquired into matters of public interest and public expense, whereas the manor court dealt with trivial matters pertaining to the locality. The sheriff's tourn and the manorial court were almost identical in object; the first was the representative of the Crown dispensing justice to the king's subjects; in a lesser radius and degree, the lord of the manor had a similar office to fulfil.

Manors were ruled by custom, and customs varied in different places. The general aspect of a court roll will always be found to be identical. The older rolls are in Latin, but, like the deeds, the later ones are written in English. The earliest ones are literally 'rolls' closely written on parch-

ment in the handwriting called by the French
' miniscule.'

Every court roll has at its commencement the
name of the manor written either above or on the
margin. The opening words read thus, 'Visus
franciplegii cum curia.' After this is the name of
the lord of the manor, the date of the day and
month, followed by the king's name and the
number of years since he ascended the throne.

Esson., on the margin, is the abbreviation for
essonium, an excuse—namely, the jurymen who
pleaded absence from the court. Following this
are the names of the twelve jurymen present, and
then the work begins.

In the older rolls the presentment of offences
are the principal items; latterly only the tenants
and their leases employed the attention of the
court at its annual sitting.

The first thing to consider was usually the
assize—licensing, so to speak, of bread and ale.
By this means fraud and adulteration were held
in check. The right of brewing ale was a privilege
not to be infringed without penalty; the fine
imposed was at the rate of 1*d*. for each illegal
brewing, the offenders are generally women.

Any damage to crops or fences, highways
needing repair, quarrels ending in bloodshed,
neglect by which animals were permitted to stray
and become seized by the hayward or pinder

All such offences are found chronicled in the court roll. Last of all is the sum total received in fines, signed by the names of the two officers appointed to superintend the assize.

A court roll is always written throughout in one handwriting, without any private marks or signatures. From the writing, they are generally the work of a professional scribe or clerk who must have had a regular education—first as a Latin scholar, secondly as an accountant, and thirdly as a writer—mistakes or erasures are seldom to be detected; therefore the rolls must have been carefully copied at leisure from rough notes made at the time; moreover, the spelling of the surnames is fairly constant, which would not be if written from dictation.

Up to the Reformation period, the court rolls were cherished as being valuable records, providing standards for future reference; hence we find, until then, a fairly perfect sequence of these yearly rolls, after which a break occurs, and only a casual roll here and there is preserved. No guide to court rolls would be complete unless the oldest form of the Arabic numerals is given and explained.

The Roman numerals are the oldest method of writing figures in Europe, but gradually the so-called Arabic figures (really of Indian origin) were introduced, superseding the former style. To

Gerbert, otherwise known as Pope Silvester II. (he died in 1003), is attributed their introduction from the East to the West; any way, from the twelfth century, the Arabic numerals rapidly came

xiith century.	xiiith century.	xivth century.	xvth century.
1.			
2.			
3.			
4.			
5.			
6.			
7.			
8.			
9.			
0.			

into use. The o was not invented before the twelfth century. A curious resemblance is traceable between the figures of the alternate centuries. Our present style of figures has grown out of the older ones, but is bolder in outline and curve. The figure 5 has passed through most variation, while 6, 8 and 9 have scarcely altered at all.

It must be remembered that before 1752, the old style was still used in England. The year therefore commenced on March 25th instead, as it does at present, of January 1st. When the calendar was corrected in 1752, eleven days were omitted, and September 2nd was followed by September 14th. The people bewailed it, and contemporary skits are numerous, echoing the popular cry of 'Give us back our lost eleven days.'

On the Continent the alteration had taken place long before. In some English parish church registers we find confusion as to the actual year date to be used for the months between Christmas and Lady Day. This uncertainty may be observed before 1750. In many country places the old style was maintained long after the year 1752.

I have a very curious old calendar of 1483; in it the saints' days are veritable red-letter days. Many of the saints named are unknown to us either by name or legend, but in court rolls only the principal saints' days are mentioned as those on which the court sat.

Some months seem to have been more favoured with saints' days than others. The following list gives the chief English saints:

January.

1. Circumcisio Domini.
13. St. Veronica.
13. St. Hilary.
25. Conversion of St. Paul.

February.

1. St. Bride, or Bridget.
2. Purification of the Virgin, or Candle-
   mas Day.
24. St. Mathias the Apostle.

March.

1. St. David.
2. St. Chad.
4. St. Lucius, Pope and Martyr, A.D. 253.
14. St. Benet, or Benedict.
18. St. Edward.
19. St. Joseph the Virgin's husband.
20. St. Cuthbert.
25. Annunciation of the Virgin. Lady-Day.

April.

23. St. George.
25. St. Mark the Evangelist.

May.

1. St. Philip and St. James the Less,
   Apostles.
2. St. Athanasius.

3. Invention (or discovery) of the Holy Cross.
5. St. Hilary, bishop of Arles. The two saints of this name are confusing, but this St. Hilary is rarely mentioned in English documents.
26. St. Augustine.

June.

11. St. Barnabas, Apostle.
13. St. Anthony of Padua.
22. St. Alban.
24. Nativity of St. John the Baptist. Midsummer Day.
29. Sts. Peter and Paul, Apostles.
30. St. Paul, Apostle.

July.

2. Visitation of the Blessed Virgin.
15. St. Swithin.
22. St. Mary Magdalen.
25. St. James the Great, Apostle.
25. St. Christopher. Lammastide.

August.

1. St. Peter ad Vincula, or St. Peter in chains.
5. St. Oswald.
6. The Transfiguration of our Lord.
15. The Assumption of the Virgin.
21. St. Bernard.

24. St. Bartholomew, Apostle.
28. St. Austin or Augustine.
29. Beheading of St. John the Baptist.

September.

1. St. Egidius, or Giles.
8. The Nativity of the Blessed Virgin.
14. Exaltation of the Holy Cross.
21. St. Matthew, Apostle and Evangelist.
29. St. Michael and All Angels. Michaelmas.

October.

4. St. Francis of Assisi.
9. St. Denis, or Dionysius of Paris.
17. St. Audry, or Etheldreda.
18. St. Luke the Evangelist.
21. St. Ursula, and 11,000 virgins.
25. St. Crispin.
28. St. Simon the Canaanite, Apostle.

November.

1. All Saints' Day.
2. All Souls' Day.
11. St. Martin. Martinmas.
16. St. Edmund.
21. Presentation of the Blessed Virgin.
22. St. Cecilia.
25. St. Catherine.
30. St. Andrew, Apostle.

December.

6. St. Nicholas.
8. The Conception of the Blessed Virgin.
13. St. Lucy.
21. St. Thomas, Apostle.
25. The Nativity of our Blessed Lord. Christmas.
26. St. Stephen.
27. St. John, Evangelist and Apostle.
28. The Holy Innocents.
29. St. Thomas à Beckett.

The saints' days were brought before the people in many ways—in the village feasts, or the dedication of churches, in the mural paintings which covered the church walls, and in the Christian names given at baptism. In the old rolls the date of the month is never mentioned, the principal feast day nearest to it being used instead.

CHAPTER VII.

MONASTIC CHARTERS.

EVERY abbey of any importance kept a chartulary, in other words, a catalogue of its
possessions in the copies of grants of land all
collected within a single volume—a carefully compiled work, giving all the benefactions and privi-
leges of the foundation, entered by the scribe or
secretary of the establishment, who must have
spent many hours of his life over the work, for these
books are rarely found to be the work of more than
one or, at most, two men—one handwriting con-
tinuing on until replaced by another. Great care
and neatness was used in the formation of each
black letter—even and perfect as the most exact
printing ever done by machinery. Each charter
was emphasized with an elaborate capital letter,
and the index or headings to them were filled in
after the writing was finished, as is proved by the

fact that these were sometimes never completed. The probability is that they were the work of another artist or illuminator, and appear to have been sketched in with a brush or hair pencil, the writing having been executed with a quill pen. Colour is sometimes employed to embellish and ornament the work, but in the oldest chartularies, colour, usually red, is only used to mark special passages, or, as in Domesday Book, to point out names of persons or places. The largest work on English monasteries was compiled by Sir William Dugdale; but in so extensive a work as the 'Monasticon,' so much was undertaken, that it was impossible to search deeply enough into existing records for information concerning every religious house throughout England. Therefore, although a valuable foundation to start with, much more may still be ascertained from manuscripts, public and private, particularly with regard to the lesser religious houses or cells to foreign abbeys.

Christianity among the Anglo-Saxons was a missionary undertaking, therefore it encouraged the foundation of centres, but these seem to have rather taken the form of bishoprics; still, information as to the early Church in England does not exist sufficiently in detail to permit us to state clearly the actual religious work or its method of working.

Later on the Saxon abbeys partook rather of

the nature of large training colleges, where learning was carried on.

The mission of St. Augustine extended the monastic system, and spread Christianity to a wider extent. It also encouraged the resort hither of foreign monks. Great rivalry existed between the English bishops and these foreign missionary priests, a feud which never seems entirely to have died out. The largest number of English abbeys sprang up after the Norman Conquest. The invaders manifested their religion by bestowing large grants of lands as votive offerings and in token of gratitude, while Duke William's honest repayment of the loans given him for the equipment of his armada brought over hundreds of priests and monks, to take possession of their new territories. Church building was a religious work often undertaken for the expiation of sins. This voluntary work was the best of its kind. To this day the remains of the old Norman abbeys surprise us with their solidity of structure and elegance of design. They must, indeed, have been beautiful when the interiors were fitted up with corresponding magnificence. At first the monks were poor—they were given land, not always of the best, often in wild and unfrequented regions; but by frugality, skill and industry, they soon brought it into a fertile state, and lived on its produce and the gifts of their patrons. The Cistercians were great wool-dealers, and we know how much English cloth was prized at home and abroad for its goodness of quality. In course of time the monks, by their labours, became rich. The need for toil being over, they sank into indolent affluence; instead of hard-working communities, they became wealthy landowners. The abbots were miniature kings, ruling over their vassals and dependents, living in almost royal state, surrounded by their court. The history of monastic England extends over very many centuries, even if its commencement is only placed at the arrival of St. Augustine in A.D. 597, or later still, with the Norman invasion.

Changes of all kinds had taken place in those long centuries. Large abbeys had sunk into poverty, and others arisen in their places. The monks had been sub-divided into orders, each having its own peculiar rules. The oldest of these was the Benedictine, or Black Monks, who held most of the largest monasteries—as many as 156 in number. From this Order arose the Cistercians, even more severe in their regulations —popular in England, probably from having had an Englishman as their founder, Stephen Harding, head of the Monastery of Citeaux (Cistercium) about the year 1125. This order had been approved by the Pope twenty-five years previously.

Gasquet gives the names of 86 Cistercian houses in England, the Cluniac as 26, and Carthusian as 9. These lesser orders had each its own distinctive rules, but, as the above figures show, were less popular than the older orders of monks. The number of nunneries was also very large (Gasquet gives 140). These were principally of the Benedictine Order. There was only one house of White Nuns in England, that of Grace Dieu, in Leicestershire.

As the old Benedictine Order relaxed its severity, the Cistercians came forward, and when these were no longer conspicuous for piety and austerity, there arose the wandering missionaries known as Friars, who were also eloquent preachers, a marked contrast to the half-educated clergy. These friars were mendicant orders, bound by oath neither to possess land or money, nor to enjoy luxury. They went about preaching throughout the country; it was the old story of the 'house divided against itself being unable to stand.' The friars preached against the monks, and the monks opposed the clergy, ending in the downfall of the three rivals under Henry VIII.

The first order of friars was of Spanish origin, founded by Dominic, A.D. 1219. They wore a brown habit of coarse hair-cloth. A few years later St. Francis of Assisi founded the Grey Friars, called after him Franciscans. These came to England A.D. 1224, where they became very popular. Like the monks, lesser orders arose out of these. The Premonstratensians gained little ground in England, but the Augustinian or Austin Friars had many followers, both men and women.

Henry VIII.'s first attack on religious houses was made upon those whose yearly incomes did not exceed £200. But the work thus begun did not end here. It is said that 376 small monasteries were doomed; of these 123 escaped immediate dissolution. Throughout 1535 and the succeeding five years, the work of suppression was carried on. During that time the monks foresaw that ultimately they were doomed, and had time to sell or hide their choicest possessions before the Commissioners appeared to claim them. Then no doubt many valuable manuscripts and papers were destroyed, or else either hidden or removed out of the country.

In several places some of these buried treasures have come to light after being concealed for a long time.

In this way a beautiful copy of the Reading Abbey Chartulary was preserved for two hundred years, having been concealed in a secret chamber adjoining a chimney-stack in an old manor-house at Shinfield, only discovered by workmen during some repairs in the last century.

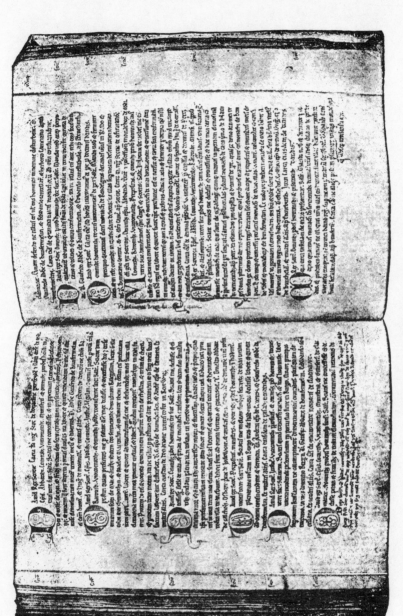

READING ABBEY CHARTER.

(Photographed by Mr. A. A. Harrison, of Theale. Kindly lent by Lord Fingal.)

This book is a good example of its kind, being perfect as the day when it was first hidden away. In it are written the grants of lands from the Abbey's second foundation by Henry I. Vast possessions given bit by bit—generally by those families whose ancestors lay buried in the abbey church, for whose souls prayers were desired. The inventories of relics are very curious, and the vestments also are described. There is a long list of the books in the abbey libraries of Reading and Leominster. All the books in this long list disappeared, no one knows where or how. Two volumes, a missal and a book of hours, said once to have been part of the abbey library, were sold by auction in 1889. Nor was Reading the only instance of the total disappearance of valuable monastic manuscripts.

Gasquet speaks of the wanton destruction of manuscripts at this period, and says that they were sold for all kinds of uses.

Mr. Maskell, 'Monumentæ Ritualiæ Ecclesiæ Anglicanæ,' reckons there must have been more than 250,000 volumes of Church service books in use, and that they must have been destroyed to prevent men from following the worship of their forefathers. A most interesting article on Ancient Prymers, the service books of the people, appeared in the *Antiquary* of March, 1892, written by Mr. Henry Littlehales.

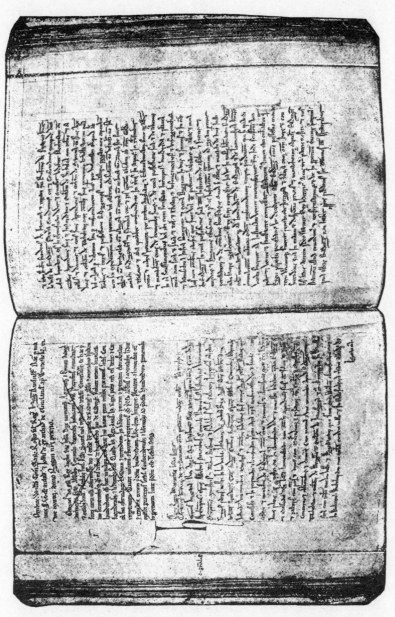

READING ABBEY CARTULARY.

(Photographed by Mr. A. A. Harrison, of Theale.)

in the *Antiquary* of March, 1892, written by Mr. Henry Littlehales.

The original deeds or grants of land to abbeys are seldom met with among private documents. The wording differs little from that of an ordinary grant, except that the donor gives for the good of his soul and the souls of his ancestors. Sometimes very interesting details may be gathered from the foundation deeds of chantries, with the appointment of a priest to celebrate Mass and offer up prayers for the dead, receiving in return a salary derived from lands or else given at once in money.

Original grants from the Crown to abbeys are seldom dated the day or year they were written; except that they conclude with the names of the bishops attesting them and the witnesses who were present, although sometimes the king's reign is given, or the episcopal year of the archbishop or diocesan bishop.

The witnesses were chosen from the king's chief officers, with a few local magnates. This will sometimes be a valuable guide to locality when the county is not named. But as a rule the name of the county is written on the margin, and also the name of the place, together with a brief index of the contents of the charter.

The names of the English archbishops and bishops are important as supplying the date of undated charters. Of the latter the contracted names of the

sees are all given in Wright's 'Court-hand Restored,'
but neither there nor in any other book is mention
made of the Norman bishops,* who frequently
appear as witnesses to monastic charters.

Bishoprics of Normandy, etc.

	NAME OF SEE.	MODERN NAME.
Archbishopric :	Rothomagensis.	Rouen.
Bishopric :	Baiocensis.	Bayeux.
,,	Abrincatensis.	Avranches.
,,	Lexoviensis.	Lisieux.
,,	Ebroicensis.	Evreux.
,,	Cadomensis.	Caen.
,,	Sylvanectensis.	Senliz.
,,	Bellovacensis.	Beauvais.
,,	Atrebatensis.	Arras.
,,	Constantiensis.	Coutances.
,,	Sagiensis.	Séez.
,,	Ambianensis or	
	Samarobrivensis.	Amiens.

As likely to be a help towards affixing the date
of undated charters I append a list of the archbishops and chancellors of England from the
Conquest; also a few of the bishops of the same
period.

Archbishops of Canterbury.

Stigand ...	...	...	1052-1070
Lanfranc	...	...	1070-1089
Anselm ...	...	...	1093-1109

* A list of French Bishops will be found in 'Gallia Christiana,'
or in 'Neustria Pia.'

Ralph of Escures	...	1114-1122
William of Corbeil	...	1123-1135
Theobald ...	...	1139-1161
Thomas à Beckett	...	1162-1170
Richard ...	...	1174-1184
Baldwin ...	...	1185-1190
Reginald Fitz Joscelin	...	1191
Hubert Walter ...	...	1193-1205
Stephen Langton	...	1205-1216-28
Richard de Grand	...	1229-1231
Edmund Rich ...	...	1234-1240
Boniface of Savoy	...	1245-1270
Robert Kilwardby	...	1273-1278
John Peckham ...	...	1279-1292
Robert Winchelsey	...	1294-1313

Next to Canterbury the second great southern
bishopric was Salisbury. The latter was a very
large and powerful diocese, commencing first at
Dorchester A.D. 634, dividing into two sees, Winchester and Sherborne, A.D. 705, which were
further subdivided, the latter into Sherborne,
Wells and Crediton, and the Winchester see into
Selsey and Ramsbury (Corvinensis); all reuniting
in 1075 into the powerful bishopric of Old Sarum,
eventually removed to Salisbury, 1218. Thus it
will be seen that Winchester and Sherborne were
the chief bishoprics, the others being offshoots of
later creation.

The Bishops of Salisbury commenced under Herman (died 1077), previously known as Bishop of Sherborne (Scirburniensis).

Osmund, died Dec. 3, 1099.

Roger, elected 1102. consecrated 1107, died 1139.

Jocelin de Bailul, died a Cistercian Monk at Waverley Abbey, 1184.

Hubert Walter, 1189, translated to Canterbury, 1193.

Herbert Poore, 1194.

Richard Poore, 1217. The see then transferred to New Sarum or Salisbury.

Robert Bingham, 1228.

William of York, 1246.

Giles de Bridport, 1256.

Walter de La Wyle, 1263.

Robert de Wykehampton, 1271.

Walter Scammel, 1284.

Henry de Braundeston, 1287.

William de La Corner, 1289.

Nicolas Longespée, 1293.

Simon of Ghent, 1297.

Roger de Mortival, 1315.

Chief Justices of England.

Odo of Bayeux and William Fitz
   Osbern, Earl of Hereford   ... 1067

William de Warren and Richard Fitz Gilbert	1073
Lanfranc, Archbishop of Canterbury, Geoffrey, Bishop of Coutances, and Robert, Count of Mortain ...	1078
Odo, Bishop of Bayeux	1087-1088
William de St. Carilepho, Bishop of Durham	1088
Ralph Flambard, Bishop of Durham	1094-1100
Robert Bloett, Bishop of Lincoln ...	1100-1107
Roger Le Poor, Bishop of Salisbury	1107-1139
Robert de Beaumont, Earl of Leicester	1154-1167
Richard de Luci	1154-1179
Ranulph Glanville	1180-1189
Hugh, Bishop of Durham, and William, Earl of Essex	1189
Hugh, Bishop of Durham, and William Longchamp, Bishop of Ely ...	1190
William Longchamp alone ...	1190
Walter of Coutances, Archbishop of Rouen	1191-1193
Hubert Walter, Archbishop of Canterbury	1193-1198
Geoffrey Fitz Peter, Earl of Essex ...	1198-1213
Peter des Roches, Bishop of Winchester	1214-1215
Hubert de Burgh...	1215-1232
Stephan Segrave	1232-1234

Hugh Bigot	...	...	...	1258-1260
Hugh Le Despenser		...	...	1260
Philip Basset	...	...	...	1261
Ralph de Hengham		...	...	1273-1289
Gilbert de Thornton		...	...	1289-1295
Roger Brabazon	...	...	...	1295

Chancellors of England.

Herfast, afterwards Bishop of Elmham	1068
Osbern, afterwards Bishop of Exeter	1070-1074
Osmond, afterwards Bishop of Salisbury	1074-1078
Maurice, afterwards Bishop of London	1078-1083
William de Beaufoe, afterwards Bishop of Thetford	1083-1085
William Giffard	1086-1090
Robert Bloett	1090
Walderic	1093
William Giffard	1094-1101
Roger Le Poor	1101-1103
William Giffard	1103-1104
Walderic	1104
Ranulph	1108-1123
Geoffrey Rufus	1124-1135
Roger Le Poor	1135-1139
Philip	1139
Thomas à Beckett	1154-1162
Ralph de Warneville	1173-1181

Geoffrey	1181-1189
William Longchamp, Bishop of Ely	1189-1197
Eustace, Bishop of Ely	1198-1199
Hubert Walter	1199-1205
Walter Grey	1205-1213
Peter des Roches	1213-1214
Walter Grey	1214
Richard de Marisco	1214-1226
Ralph Neville	1226-1244
Walter de Merton	1261
Nicolas de Ely	1263
Thomas Cantelupe	1265
Walter Giffard	1265
Godfrey Giffard	1267
Richard Middleton	1269-1272
Walter de Merton	1272
Robert Burnell	1273-1292
John Langton	1292
William Greenfield	1302
William of Hamilton	1304
Ralph Baldock	1307

CHAPTER VIII.

PARISH REGISTERS.

THE study of parish registers is quite apart from that of old deeds. The writing of the former begins at the period where the latter usually end, for deeds written in the seventeenth century are regarded by the antiquary as modern; but then comes the most difficult handwriting of all to decipher, because the old race of scholarly clerks had died out and been replaced by less educated men.

Parish registers are unique in many ways. They contain information nowhere else obtainable. Sometimes, besides the mere repetition of names, there are inserted scraps of original information, for the clergyman had undisputed possession of the volumes, which remained usually in the keeping of his deputy, the parish clerk, and either of them could enter in the books whatever he pleased.

Every now and then an outcry arises as to the

condition and care of parish registers, and desire is
expressed that they should be deposited in a large
public office similar to the Public Record Office; but
anyone who has wished to make or obtain extracts
from the registers at the diocesan registries is
well aware of the trouble and expense involved;
search fees soon mount up, nor can careful preservation be ensured by any such an arrangement.   Many are the known instances where the
precious volumes have been purposely mutilated,
or by neglect suffered to fall into decay and illegi-
bility; but, as a whole, it is wonderful to see the
excellent condition and preservation of these old
records, which, if once removed out of their own
parishes into a large public collection, would lose
all individuality, and become merged in the mass
of manuscripts which are more or less buried in
every large library.

It is a pity that some arrangement cannot be
made to ensure preservation by a few copies
being printed of each register ; the work is
gradually being undertaken privately, but ought
to be worked on a more systematic plan with
uniformity throughout England.

An order such as this would not in any way
affect the fees accruing to the clergy from re-
searches, but rather tend to increase them, for at
present much information is lost because its where-
abouts is unknown.   It is this question of search-

fees which causes such a steady resistance on the part of the resident clergy to any such project. But in spite of this, the work has been begun already; the registers of many parishes are printed, or have MS. transcripts all ready for the press, nor is the expense as great as might be imagined; a few copies unbound may be produced at a cost of from £3 to £10, in proportion to the amount of matter to be printed.

It is not unusual, when applying by letter for extracts from an old register, to receive a reply of apology from the clergyman recommending a personal search on the part of the inquirer, as the information could not be sent owing to inability to read the unfamiliar old handwriting. This would be avoided if a printed copy properly indexed were at hand for reference, while on any important matter, where an attested copy from the original was necessary, it could be obtained as heretofore.

The history of parish registers commences from the Reformation year of 1536. What previous system had existed we are unable to say, for information on the subject is lacking. Here and there fragments of registers are known earlier than the above quoted date, but these are the exception, not the rule. Deaths noted down by the chantry priests or monks, are found on the margins of old monastic breviaries, where prayers for the souls of the departed had been desired.

The subject is one of vast importance, for without proper registration, it is impossible to decide the legality of a marriage, or prove legitimacy of offspring, both necessary points of law where inheritance of landed property is concerned.

The scheme of parochial registration, as devised by Henry VIII.'s shrewd minister Cromwell, was only copied from a like plan long in use abroad.

The idea at first, being new to the English people, met with much opposition, being mistaken for a new species of taxation; but, nevertheless, it was ordered to be carried out under penalty of fines, and, being found a valuable institution, was submitted to, until custom fully established it. Thus the old parish registers cannot be older than 1536, except in very exceptional cases. But the order did not become general till two years later, therefore 1538 may be reckoned as the year when they may be said to have in reality begun.

At first the books were carefully written, the entries being in Latin. After awhile less care was taken. The notes were made on rough strips of paper called ' clerk's notes,' and were supposed to be entered at fixed intervals in the book; but often this was irregularly performed, and the strips were mislaid and lost before they could be copied. In some parishes, both the clerk's notes as well as the old register book may still be seen and compared. The religious uncertainty of the succeeding reigns caused the question of registration to be ignored, but Queen Elizabeth issued several commands on the subject, notably that by which transcripts were yearly sent at Easter to be preserved among the diocesan records.

Most of the old parish register books now existing are transcripts made according to this command, as can be seen at a glance, for the handwriting is uniform throughout, which could not have been the case if the notes made by the clerk had been periodically copied into the book. Another more stringent Act, to ensure yearly copies being made, was passed upon James I.'s accession to the throne, and the clergyman's name was to be affixed to each page as witness that the copy was faithfully exact. Had these wise regulations been carried out to the letter and in the spirit that was intended, we should now possess an invaluable corroboration of the accuracy of the parish registers ; but alas, the transcripts to be found in the diocesan registries are meagre and imperfect. Years and series of years are missing, and the entries are so lacking in detail as to be practically useless.

Personal search can of course be made among the diocesan registers, and this is strongly to be recommended, for any mistakes in a transcript render it not only valueless, but mischievous, for extracts from registers are the most dangerous material a genealogist has to deal with. For unless further authenticated by wills and old deeds to confirm the relationship, it will be found no easy job to piece together these broken links in the chain of evidence, and without wilful misrepresentation being intended, mistakes may and will occur.

Take, for instance, any name, and try to trace out the pedigree with the help of the parish register only. At first it is easy enough, whether worked backwards or forwards, but after the first three or four generations have been worked out, all certainty of relationship is lost, and becomes confused.

The handwriting of the parish registers is a combination of the old set law-hand and the personal handwritings mentioned in the second chapter. Original entries (*i.e.*, entries made at the time of performing the religious ceremony) are seldom met with before the middle of James I.'s reign, by which time the Latin language had fallen into disuse.

The Commonwealth Government passed an Act of Parliament appointing paid registrars to every village (1653). These were illiterate men, whose only accomplishments consisted of being

able to read and write, and whose zeal and discretion alone regulated the keeping of the register
books. This duty was often but ill-performed,
especially when age and infirmity overtook the
registrar, who continued in office until death
relieved him of his duties. No second registrar
seemed in any case to have been appointed, and
the work of keeping the registers devolved again
upon the clergyman and his assistant clerk.

For several years after the Restoration of 1660,
the registers were irregularly kept, and very
erratic. The old race of educated clerks was gone.
Formerly, when the registers first began, clerk-
ships may have been filled by men educated in the
monasteries, who, when turned adrift, were glad
to employ themselves as priests' chaplains or
private tutors as a means of livelihood.

Until this century no small schools of any kind
existed for the poorer classes, except those provided by charitable bequests. These were few and
far between, and could be of little benefit to the
masses of the people. No wonder, then, that
the ill-paid clergy were obliged to be content with
very uneducated men to serve in the capacity of
clerk. The registers of the latter part of the
seventeenth century are indited in every variety
of illegibly bad writing.

The chief difficulty of reading the old registers
lies in the immense variety of forms a name was

capable of passing through, owing to the laxity of
English spelling and pronunciation. The people
knew their own surnames only by oral tradition,
and were entirely dependent upon the parish
clerk, who wrote down the name as it sounded to
him, and as sounds have a different effect on
different persons, the commonest names often
appeared in very strange and unrecognisable dis-
guises before they finally crystallized into their
modern forms.

It is not unusual to find items of miscellaneous
information jotted down at random by the clergyman among the entries of births, marriages, and
deaths. Heavy falls of snow, disastrous floods,
periods of drought, storms of any kind, were all
events of great local importance in country places,
and would remain for a long time as traditional
landmarks in their annals. Alas, such items are
rare, and are now rendered impossible in the
printed pages of the modern register books.

The most useful and least troublesome way to
catalogue the contents of a parish register for
reference, is to write out the year, and below it
enter the births, marriages, and deaths, with the
names occurring under each heading, but without
taking the time or trouble to copy the dates of
day or month, these last being only required for
law investigations, and for which purpose the
originals only would be received as evidence.

Parliamentary blue-books have been issued on the subject of parochial registers, and a most useful handbook is now in course of preparation, giving as complete a catalogue as possible of all registers of which printed copies or indexes have been made up to the present day.

CHAPTER IX.

PARISH OFFICERS AND THEIR BOOKS.

AMONG the contents of the parish deed-chest wherein registers are supposed to be safely kept, are often found other books and papers, seemingly of little interest or importance, but in reality very likely to yield curious and original scraps of information, with glimpses into the life of the poorer classes during the past centuries. Some day these old account-books, now flung aside as worthless, will be of great importance in an antiquary's eyes, for they give lists of all the residents in the parish, from the squire to the lowest and poorest, showing the social status of each; and further, are of value when compared with the parish registers, as giving a clue to the length of residence of inhabitants who, if of the middle class, sooner or later served their turn as parish officers; and if paupers, were entered as recipients of parochial charity.

Previous to this century, the churchwardens, overseers, road surveyors and parish constables held office for one year only, being elected at the annual Easter vestry ; now re-election is supposed to take place, but the post is carried on from year to year without opposition.

Apparently some rule of yearly income or rental governed the election, or else certain tenements were represented in rotation by their tenants, for widows were liable to serve, in which case a son or some near neighbour was deputed to act in the woman's name.

Now the custom of yearly change has died out, and a churchwarden once elected goes on from year to year, until sickness, old age, or death renders some fresh arrangement absolutely necessary. Surely, if in those old days, when education was so sparsely distributed, and even reading and writing looked upon as sciences—if then it was possible to find men able and capable of directing local affairs, it seems strange that now so few are considered fit for the post, when every day-labourer's son is taught drawing and essay-writing in addition to his elementary studies.

The office of churchwarden is very old. Now it has lost most of its prestige, and the church-warden is almost forgotten except on the Sundays when collections are made ; but formerly each villager took a personal interest in affairs which some day he himself would probably be called upon to manage.

The two churchwardens of a parish represented the rival interests of its inhabitants; the parson *versus* the squire and his tenants. Each officer had his clients' interests to uphold and consider. The most onerous duty, however, fell upon the overseer of the poor, in whose hands rested the responsibility of the proper distribution of the public funds in the shape of bequests and legacies; to him came applications for relief, and with him also were mooted all questions relating to the disposal of paupers, both dead and alive. Edward III. forbade the giving of alms to able-bodied men, but no regular poor laws were invented till Henry VIII. was king.

The first Acts of Parliament relating to poor laws were passed towards the conclusion of Queen Elizabeth's long reign. It was absolutely necessary to make some fresh statutes applicable to the new state of affairs consequent upon the Reformation. Previously all charity had been distributed or directed by the monks, and after they were dispersed and their lands seized by the Crown and sold, their unfortunate dependents were rendered still more dependent, and all the severe laws against vagrancy and beggars made by the Tudor sovereigns could not abate the nuisance or solve the difficult question, while doles and gifts

of bread or alms served only to increase the evil
through toleration.

Worse and worse the state of things became,
till towards the end of the last century the climax
was reached; there were then whole families of
paupers who, generation after generation, made
no effort towards self-support either for themselves or their offspring. These last were brought
up entirely on charity, clothed, fed and appren-
ticed, till finally married by charity, the fees being
paid out of the charity money; nor did the matter
end there, for, probably, after the lapse of years
the wedded couple with their children (if they
became chargeable to the parish) were returnel
to their native village, again to become recipients
of its charity till death claimed them, and the
parish paid the funeral expenses.

The first commission upon the poor laws took
place in William IV.'s reign, and since then
reform has gradually been at work. In many
places public charity is still abused; but no real
good can be effected at once, and every effort
must be proved by long and fair trial, under
which all unsuitable experiments will fail, and
only the practical and beneficial ones will survive
the test. Of course, all relief and outdoor assistance was left very much to the discretion and
honesty of the overseer, whose accounts were
yearly scrutinized at the Easter vestry, when most

parochial accounts were discussed. Sometimes these discussions were considered of sufficient importance to be entered in the parish books. Questions as to the ownership and distribution of pews in the church, repairs to the edifice, by whom they were to be done, boundaries, and whose business it was to keep in order certain roads lying between rival parishes—all such matters came forward for consideration, and, finally, the officers for the ensuing year were elected, and the books handed over to the new churchwardens.

Perhaps a further check upon miscellaneous entries being made in the books was that all the accounts had 'to be passed' at the nearest Sessions and signed by the presiding magistrate, who was some neighbouring squire.

The parish constable is now replaced by the policeman supplied by the county, the visible representative of the law in rural places.

One entry often found among the old accounts was of repairs done to the village stocks, frequently used to punish petty offences, especially drunkenness. The pound, too, often needed mending; fines for allowing animals to stray and become empounded are among the most frequent entries in old manor court rolls. In many places a hayward was a regularly appointed officer for this purpose, whose duty it was to capture the animals and attend to them until they were reclaimed by their owner or sold to defray expenses. In Berkshire the hayward, or pinder, gave a tally to the person who brought the beast found on his land, and he did not deliver the beast until its owner produced the tally, proving that compensation for damage had been properly paid.

The offices of overseer of the poor and of road surveyor, formerly called waywarden, are not of any great antiquity; nor are they of great consequence so far as regards the old account books, in which their elections are often not even mentioned. As to the constable, we only get a casual glimpse of his duties when we read a list of his expenses incurred in conveying some delinquent parishioner to the county gaol, or of journeys taken to distant places to inquire into the antecedents of paupers or in taking them back to their own villages.

It is the overseers' accounts which are really curious, those long lists of garments bought to clothe the paupers and their children, the old apprentice forms by which the children were placed out in service so soon as they were capable of earning a stray sixpence towards their own keep; cruel as it seemed to be to send out such young children to work, it was, in reality, the kindest thing that could be done for them, for it gave them a chance of becoming independent and working for themselves.

Maybe a bundle of old papers are rolled together among the account books. These may be the orders for the removal of paupers back to the village they called ' home,' a custom first originated by some Acts of Parliament passed by Charles II. At the same time the parish officers were commanded and forced by penalties to provide for paupers removed back into their parish, and, to prevent fraud, written proofs as to the proper home or residence of the paupers had to be obtained and produced; these papers are called ' settlements.'

The officers did their best for the welfare of their charges : they provided the old women with spinning-wheels, so that they could earn a trifle for themselves, while the men were set to work on the road; when failing in health they were tended by a parish nurse, and if sick the doctor saw them. Sometimes they were sent to Bath or Cheltenham to be cured by the far-famed waters. For many years these old annuitants lingered on, till we read the last entry paid for burying Goody or Goodman So-and-so.

Any public event which required to be celebrated by the ringing of the church bells is sure to be mentioned among the ordinary expenses.

There are in the old books (those of that unsettled time when the religion of the State varied according to the sovereign in power, during the Tudor and Stuart dynasties) many notices of the alterations wrought both in town and country places. The church goods were first catalogued by order of Edward VI.'s ministers; rich vestments, altar hangings, and numerous vessels are named in the first list, but later on, under Queen Elizabeth, the parish churches were further despoiled, till there was little left for the Puritans to remove, and in the later lists only the old service books and books of religious instruction are left to the churchwardens to chronicle. Although instances as early as 1287 are on record, the erection of pews was an innovation only introduced by degrees after the Reformation. The destruction of screens and the removal of altars caused altar rails and communion tables to be used instead. Then came the terrors of civil war. Upon the churchwardens devolved the duty of providing burial for soldiers slain in battle. Such burials were not often in the churchyard, but on the boundaries of parishes, the expenses being defrayed equally; this was probably an old custom in warfare, but it was carried out as late as the Commonwealth. A battle was a public calamity, and the responsibility of providing interment for the slain was therefore a public duty.

After the Restoration the churches were repaired and the royal arms restored.   Later on we find some parsons resigning their work from nonconforming scruples; at this time, too, are notices of excommunicated persons.   The Puritan zeal was aroused by James II.'s injudicious attempt to restore Catholicism; and attendance at church, first commanded by Queen Elizabeth, was further enforced by an order that taking of the Sacrament should be regarded as a test of conformity; for disobedience the punishment of excommunication was inflicted upon the churchwardens' application to the bishop.   The Recusants, as papists were called, were treated with great severity and injustice.

Any fresh Act of Parliament with reference to fees or taxes was soon noted in the parish books. Fees varied in different places, according to custom.   Prior to the eighteenth century fees for burial within the church were payable to the churchwardens, but afterwards became the parson's perquisite.   These entries may lead to the identification of vaults and interments otherwise forgotten.   The burial of strangers was always charged for at a higher rate; for paupers the parish paid the expenses, and the tax of 3d. on each burial was not enforced.   Taxes were levied on many things under the Georges, but none were more obnoxious to the people than the birth, marriage, and death taxes, of which the clergyman was made to act as a most unwilling tax-gatherer.

The window-tax fell heavily on old manor houses pierced with innumerable windows and skylights. It was then that many windows were blocked up to avoid payment.

In the last century are many entries of payment for the release of men seized for service in the army or navy; for when the father of a family went away, his wife and children were left to be provided for by charity, and the first payment by the churchwardens for his release was in the end the cheapest.

A list of rails (spelt usually 'rayles') surrounding the churchyard reminds one of another almost obsolete custom, that of each person repairing the rail in the fence next to his property or for which he was liable. The liability was attached to the land, though custom decided whether the owner or the occupier was the person to do such repairs.

Last, not least, in the parish chest were bundles of old papers, technically known as 'briefs.' In the account-books all Church collections were duly entered. Originally these were more of the nature of voluntary rates, for the name of each donor is given and the sum he gave, varying in accordance with his social position and means.

The origin of church collections is obscure; no doubt the offerings given at the sacrament were always devoted to the relief of poverty and distress.

To regulate and restrict the right of levying collections, Acts of Parliament were passed, and no collection was allowed to be made without a proper license called a 'brief'; but the issuing of these grew to an alarming extent. Briefs were issued for all sorts of emergencies and disasters, principally for damage by fire, there being then no insurance offices; and the old buildings, once set alight, were seldom rescued from total demolition. A complete list of early briefs would be curious, but would be so extensive as to fill a large volume.

The churchwardens probably kept few if any accounts prior to the sixteenth century, therefore any older church collections are unrecorded or only mentioned by chance.

In an old parish book of Sulhamstead are entries of the following collections :

1670. Collected towards the redemption of English captives in Turkey ; and again, in 1680, a similar collection took place.

It puzzled me much why such a small Berkshire parish should subscribe so liberally for the release of slaves ; but this was explained on discovering that Turkish pirates infested the seas, and even landed with impunity on the western coasts, and carried off prisoners, both men and women, to become slaves. The main road to the West ran through Berkshire; travellers along it doubtless brought tales of such wild deeds, which lost nothing in the telling, and excited the sympathy of the countryfolk.

In 1699 money was again collected; this time to redeem 300 captives detained by the King of Morocco.

In 1678 funds were collected towards the rebuilding of St. Paul's Cathedral, destroyed twelve years previously in the great fire of London. Many papists, all over England, added their contributions to this collection.

1699. Collection was made for the French refugees and Vaudois settled in Switzerland, who had fled at the revocation of the Edict of Nantes. To inhabitants of Sulhamstead village this may have had a keener interest, in that Samuel Morland, afterwards made a baronet, the son of a former rector, Rev. Thomas Morland, was sent out by Government in 1655 to inquire into the condition of the Waldenses, and he wrote thereon a book descriptive of the country and its inhabitants. Martin Morland, another son of the rector, had returned to his old home for awhile, when, at the Restoration, he resigned his living in 1665, for here two of his sons were born.

1687. Brief for loss by fire in Aylesford.

1689. Loss by fire at Bishops Lavington, Wilts.
1690. Ditto, East Smithfield.
Town of Stafford.
Town of Bungay, Suffolk.
1690. In the parish of St. George's, in the borough of Southwark.
In the Town of St. Ives, Huntingdonshire.

Five collections for fires in different counties, made in one small parish within a year.

In 1703, brief for refugees in the Principality of Orange.

After 1703 the givers' names are no longer entered.

The parish doctor was regularly engaged by the churchwardens. In 1774 the agreement for Sulhamstead was made and signed by the doctor, and witnessed that he 'should do the business of surgery and apothecary, broken bones excepted, for the yearly sum of five guineas'! No wonder that these hard-worked physicians lacked skill, and relied more upon practice than education for what talent they did possess.

The perambulation of parish bounds was another vestry question, upon which rested disputed tithes. In entries of tithe, old field-names, now forgotten, may often be recovered. The commutation of tithe also was discussed, and in some places the parson made agreements with his parishioners on the subject. Visitation fees came before the vestry, and sending copies of the register to the Diocesan Registry was, or ought to have been, an annual occurrence. Any dispute seems to have come within the vestry's jurisdiction, and all dry subjects were washed down with plenty of ale, an item regularly entered among the expenses.

Perhaps it was at the vestry that the village urchins came up to claim rewards offered for the extermination of vermin, their instinctive love of sport being further developed by their love of gain. Foxes are among the animals named on the list, together with stoats, sparrows, etc., and the prices paid for this wholesale destruction seem very high.

The spelling of many of the old account books is decidedly phonetic and original, but as a whole they are legible and neatly kept. They need nothing to explain their meanings, except a guide such as I have endeavoured to give, as to what class of information their pages will yield, for the books of one parish closely resemble all others.

CHAPTER X.

BOOKS ON PALEOGRAPHY AND KINDRED SUBJECTS.

PART of a guide-book's business is to direct people's attention to other similar works likely to be of use to them.

Few accomplishments can be learnt with the aid of only one book on the subject, and paleography is a combination of many elements. Few English writers have expended their genius in books on handwriting; it has not in this country been looked upon as one of the sciences. Abroad the subject has been more studied, especially by the French, in whose language many valuable books on it have been compiled. The type required for the abbreviations is expensive; small editions only were issued, and many valuable works are in consequence rare and little known, being only met with in public libraries or among collections of old books. Thus seventeen volumes of 'La Bibliothèque de l'Ecole des Chartres,' published in Paris between the years 1839 and 1886, will fetch as much as £30; 'Album de la Paleographie' (Quantin, 1887), £6; 'Elements de la Paleographie,' par Natalis de Wailly, two volumes, 1838, £3 3s.; 'Musée des Archives Nationales,' 1872, £1 10s.

A very useful book, less expensive than the above, was written by Prou, published in Paris by Alphonse Picard, editeur, 82, Rue Bonaparte; and cheaper still than this is the 'Paleographie des Chartes et des Manuscrits du XI. au XVII. Siècles,' par Alphonse Chassant, published by Auguste Aubry, Rue Dauphine 16, Paris. The best known cheap book on the subject, however, is a small paper-bound volume, 'Dictionnaire des Abbréviations Latines et Françaises,' par Alphonse Chassant, published by Jules Martin, 19, Boulevard Haussmann, Paris, at the low price of 2 francs 50 centimes; it has already reached a fifth edition.

There are also books on paleography written in German, Spanish and Italian, but these are seldom met with in England.

Now let us see what our own countrymen have done towards elucidating our national manuscripts. The list will not be a long one.

It must be borne in mind that first of all four separate languages are required, namely, Anglo-Saxon, Norman-French, Latin and Old English.

For the first of these, the standard work is Bosworth's Anglo-Saxon Dictionary; a second-hand copy may be bought for 8s. 6d. It contains the alphabet and grammatical peculiarities of the Anglo-Saxon language, besides the dictionary of words.

For Norman-French, all that is required at first start is a familiarity with the modern language. Any good, old-fashioned dictionary will be of assistance, and later on Roquefort's dictionary, Lacombe's Burguy, and the glossary in the Supplement to Ducange, may be resorted to, to solve difficulties.

Latin and English may be studied together, the one being translated verbatim from the other.

The standard English work upon handwriting as a whole is called 'The Origin and Progress of Handwriting,' by Astle; it was published in the beginning of this century. A good copy is now worth two or three sovereigns. This book deals with every kind of known writing from its earliest existence. There are facsimiles of Hebrew, Sanscrit, Greek, Latin, and other languages, besides specimens of English charters of each century.

The Paleographic Society was started in 1873, and their yearly volumes contain exact representations of the old documents, but these cost £1 1s. each. They are valuable as having the facsimile and its transcript side by side, but as yet they have only selected very old charters, not considering mediæval English deeds worthy of consideration. Bosworth's Anglo-Saxon dictionary is the standard work on this subject.

Some Anglo-Saxon manuscripts were published in 1878 by command of the Queen, upon the recommendation of the Master of the Rolls, the work being undertaken by General Cameron, director of the Ordnance Survey, with translations added by W. Basevi-Saunders. The charters selected were those among the archives of Canterbury Cathedral, as they give three centuries of Anglo-Saxon history, A.D. 742 to A.D. 1049. This work now fetches £2 2s.

A collection of early Anglo-Saxon charters, those of Abingdon Abbey, has been issued in the 'Rolls Series' in two volumes.* Other Anglo-Saxon documents have been printed and translated at various times.

Domesday Survey has been reproduced by a photographic process, and is extremely clear and well executed; it is also published in four volumes in a more readable type, but still abbreviated. Each county can be obtained in a separate volume. The translations are not given; this for the student is rather an advantage than otherwise.

No subject has been more studied than Domesday Book. Translations, explanations

---

* This also contains a good glossary of Anglo-Saxon words.

and dictionaries have been written upon it.
These are very valuable as explaining the obscure
points and giving the modern acreage, as compared with the carucate, bovate and hide. To
understand a county history these must be closely
compared. Many of the manors named in the
old Survey are now lost. It must be remembered
that waste lands and commons were not always
mentioned, nor were churches or any property
which was not taxable. For this reason Domesday often disappoints us by its meagreness of
detail, but it forms the beginning or basis from
which an inquiry may be started, and to pursue
it through the centuries which followed, the
public rolls and manuscripts are the only means
of information; of these Domesday will prove
valuable as a key. The really practical book on
writing best known and most popular, because
neither complicated nor expensive, is Wright's
'Court-hand Restored,' price £1, compiled in
1846 to meet a long-felt want, for Latin having
ceased as the law language, lawyers no longer
were obliged to know old legal forms and words
as part of their profession, although they often
felt the need of understanding them where
any search through old deeds was requisite.
Since then, this book has passed through nine
editions, the last of which was brought out in
1879, edited and improved by Mr. C. T. Martin,

of the Public Record Office. It contains alphabets
in all styles, facsimiles of all classes of English
writing, with translations, a glossary of obsolete
words and place-names, supplying a valuable text-
book to paleography, giving the reader all the
information necessary for studying old deeds.
Since then (1892) Mr. Martin has compiled a
fuller and more elaborate glossary, called 'The
Record Interpreter,' 10s. 6d. The amateur will
need no other books if he is provided with these
two volumes. A list of abbreviations taken from
the Pipe Rolls was issued among the yearly
volumes of the Pipe Rolls Society, price 12s. 6d.
The fourth volume of 'The Registrum Palatinum
Dunelmense,' edited by the late Sir Thomas
Duffus Hardy, in the Rolls series of ' Chronicles
and Memorials,' also contains a list of contracted
words and their explanations. Its price is 10s. 6d.

The study of old deeds brings in its train a
multiplicity of other subjects bearing upon old
customs and legal formulæ, some of which were
complicated. All the writers upon the law explain
these formalities; ' though now antiquated so far
as the actual law work and procedure is concerned,' they give the ancient methods; of these
' Blackstone's Commentaries ' is the best known.

Jacobs' ' Law Dictionary ' is another similar
book; also ' A New Law Dictionary,' by J.
Nicholson. But these books are now out of date;

they may by chance be met with at sales or on bookstalls, where they may be bought for a few shillings. Perhaps an advertisement in the *Exchange and Mart* might be successful in obtaining replies. Of guides to various branches of archæology there are plenty lately issued since the subject became fashionable.

'Record Searching,' by W. Rye, gives a glimpse into the various public collections, and the class of information likely to be derived from manuscripts.

'How to write the History of a Family,' by Phillimore, is a similar work, useful to genealogists.

'How to write the History of a Parish,' by J. C. Cox, LL.D.

The information contained in all these three last books might be with advantage remodelled and extended.

Upon Parish Registers a charming little book, full of information, has been written by Mr. Chester Waters, price 3s. 9d. Every clergyman should possess a copy of it. On Church History there are recently published two very good 1s. volumes, called 'Illustrated Notes on English Church History,' by Rev. Arthur Lane; small engravings of all the English cathedrals and many handsome and celebrated churches are given, but no descriptions of them. A very good series of

Diocesan Histories has been brought out by
the Society for Promoting Christian Knowledge.
These may now be bought second-hand at 1s. per
volume.

For derivation of words, there is no better guide
than Taylor's ' Words and Places,' and Edmunds'
' Place-names'; both these are trustworthy, and
have become recognised authorities.

Quality rather than quantity should be the
antiquary's motto in his choice of a library, but
antiquarianism and archæology require many
books of reference, and it is well to know those
books most likely to be of permanent use instead
of wasting room upon volumes not required after
the first reading. Upon Manor Rolls there is a
very clever work lately issued by the Selden
Society (volume ii.). It gives much new information on Manorial Customs. All the three volumes
issued by this society are very interesting. They
are edited by F. W. Maitland. Upon Monastic
History there are many very interesting books,
mostly published by Burns and Oates, London.

A list of useful books might be extended in-
definitely, especially if brought up to date.
Archæology is a cumulative science gleaned from
varied sources. The antiquary usually is possessed of more brains than money, but if he is
fortunate enough to possess both, a large library
will be to him a never-ending source of amusement.

CHAPTER XI.

OLD LETTERS.

THERE were always two divisions of hand-writing; the formal hand, employed for clerk's work, and a freer, less mechanical, less careful style, used for private correspondence. Writing was a profession, and, as late as the sixteenth century, when it was necessary to communicate with persons at a distance, a professional scribe was employed to write the letter. But letter-writing was rare, and did not become general till after the sixteenth century; even then it was restricted to the upper classes of society. I have in Chapter IV. given a brief account of the paper used in England. Letter or post paper was made of a square, uniform sheet, folded; it was known as 'Pot paper,' from its water-mark. This varied slightly, the jug or water-pot being much more elaborate in some examples. It came principally from abroad, either the Low Countries or Germany; each separate factory very likely adopted a distinct shape; the makers' initials are to be found upon the band across the pot, but are difficult to read.

The three following marks are taken from some old letters, and are good types of their kind.

The writing of old letters I have placed after

(1561)   (1563)   (1623)

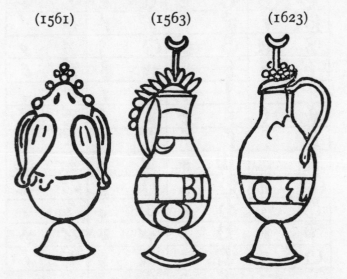

the chapter on registers, because the latter forms a link between the clerical and personal handwritings. The letters have changed entirely from the old black-letter style to a similar style, like that still in use in Germany, and assuming a distinct character, as may be seen in the following alphabet.

Therefore, not only was the material for letter-writing (*i.e.*, paper) of foreign manufacture, but

Set Chancery	Common Chancery	Court Hand	Secretary (Stuart Period)

also the handwriting bore close resemblance to foreign styles. This may have resulted from the original Anglo-Saxon element in the nationality of the people, aided by the constant immigration of merchants from the Low Countries, who came over to England during the fourteenth and fifteenth centuries, and established various branches of trade, chiefly in linen or woollen goods. They naturally introduced also the fashions and customs of their own nations. Added to this was the marriage of the king, Richard II. with the German Princess Anne of Bohemia, followed closely by the religious zeal of the Reformers, bringing Germans and German ideas strongly to the fore in English politics. The earliest printers were German, and about the time of this invention the small letter e written backwards first came into use. Unfortunately very little private correspondence exists prior to the reign of Queen Elizabeth, except that preserved among public manuscripts. In those days lifelong imprisonment was often the result of a thoughtless committal of ideas into tangible form. Letters were dangerous witnesses, and as such were destroyed as soon as read. The posts were not safe from inspection; spies were employed freely on all sides, and men, not afraid to suffer for their opinions, nevertheless did not care to risk their necks by needless imprudence.

The earliest newspapers had a blank column left to be filled by the sender with the latest intelligence or local news. These were fitly called 'News letters.' The phraseology of a seventeenth century letter seems to us strange on account of the conjugation of the verbs, the use of 'hath' in place of 'has,' and the absence of all unnecessary adverbs: the sentences, too, are longer. The commencing words and the final winding up of letters have both changed in the past two hundred years.

With the eighteenth century we see these changes gradually settling down and altering into the modern forms. The old English yᵉ for 'the,' and the abbreviated & for 'and,' and the ƀ (d) written in its antiquated shape, still remain, but the German letters by degrees are given up.

The writing of each generation is most distinctly marked; the dates from it may be approximately fixed without any difficulty, as well as the age and character of the writer.

It has been said that the introduction of cheap postage, and the immense increase of everyday correspondence, has ruined handwriting, and banished for ever the art of composition. True, the short letters of to-day will not bear comparison with the neat, voluminous diary-letters, full of graphic scenic descriptions, which our grandparents were wont to compile for the benefit of relations left at home; now, when similar correspondence is undertaken, it is copied out by the type-writer or printed, for few people will take the trouble to read manuscript compositions. Looking beyond the opening years of this century, we see a marked paucity of ideas and carelessness of caligraphy in the correspondence, getting worse the further back we go. In the seventeenth century men were the chief correspondents : they wrote on matters of business; few letters are preserved except on such topics, which is a pity, for a letter must always be a unique production, the best evidence procurable of the writer and his times.

There is little to be said on the subject of old letters. Practice in reading them makes the lettering familiar, and gives facility which no guide-book on them could explain, and letters, both ancient and modern, will assume a new interest when the little trifling, characteristic peculiarities of the writer are examined by their aid.

Old receipts, expense-books, and farm accounts are found in plenty among old papers; but what we should prize now would be descriptions of people and places as they existed some hundreds of years ago.

CHAPTER XII.

ABBREVIATIONS, ETC.

IN most books treating of ancient hand-writing, the abbreviations and contractions are put forward as the most important part; certainly it is necessary to study them carefully, but it was never intended by the old scribes that they should be regarded as a language in themselves. At first they were used to save time and space, then, by degrees, they increased in multiplicity as well as complexity, till banished altogether by the invention of printing, upon the advance of which the professional scribe disappeared.

The contracted words most frequently used are not always necessary to the sense of the sentence, which may be arrived at without them. It is a waste of time to puzzle over a word after its meaning has been arrived at. Many persons who require MS. extracts from public offices

take rough notes with the letters of the contracted word; these can be extended afterwards
at home, when there is time to seek in dictionaries for the abbreviation or its meaning; with
practice the opening words of a sentence will very
often supply the context. The oldest forms of
contraction are a straight line over a word or a
curve, these indicate that a portion of the word
only is present, but no clue is given as to the
letters left out, or else the straight line may mean
m or *n*.

Later on the straight line above a word came
to represent the letters *m* and *n*. In words
where these letters were duplicated the second
one was omitted and the line placed above to
indicate its absence. This continued in use
until late in the eighteenth century. Com͠on
meant 'common,' and com͠endation 'commenda-
tion.' If a curved line was over the end syllable
of a word, it meant one or more letters omitted at
the end of the word.

Verbs are the most troublesome class of contracted words, for a contraction over a verb
may mean any syllable, according to the proper
grammatical conjugation. Here it is that knowledge of the Latin grammar is a necessity. The
meaning of the sentences may often be de-
ciphered, without extending the words, and the
correct conjugation of the verbs can be added

afterwards by another person, if the student's knowledge of Latin is too limited to accomplish this with accuracy. Certain signs or contractions are fairly constant in their meanings, always taking the place of special syllables. Thus a bold apostrophe above the line will be found to indicate ' er,' ' ir,' ' or,' ' re.'

= ur.

ʒ = et, us. In Domesday ' et ' is written ⁊.

Ꝁ = ram, ras, ris.

ƈ = is.

⁹ = us, ous, os.

A small letter over a word shows that a syllable is left out of which this letter formed part.

The letter ' p ' had a system of its own, frequently used in old deeds and also in old letters :

p = per, par, por.

ꝑ = pre.

ꝓ = pro.

In old court rolls ' and ' is written '˜t,' and ' est ' appears as ' ÷,' especially in court-hand law deeds.

A line drawn through the head of the letter ' ł ' means also the addition of other letters, as *is*, *e*, etc. This contraction in names is apt to be confused with double ' tt.'

It is said that our alphabet did not formerly contain as many letters as at present. The letters ' i ' and ' j ' were identical until a recent period. ' W ' is said to have been derived from two ' u's,' and is always so written in old deeds, joined together, while ' u ' and ' v ' were used indiscriminately. In old manuscripts the short-stroke letters were formed alike; thus ' n,' ' u,' ' w,' ' i,' are merely strokes or minims, difficult to distinguish, more particularly where any of these letters occur side by side in the formation of words; to count the strokes is the only guide. Practice and a knowledge of likely words to be employed solve the knotty point.

The chief difficulty of all lies in the correct rendering of names, for these have perpetually changed in their spelling. In a single deed several different forms may be observed, the result of clerical copying. Even with names the system of abbreviation was carried on, especially among court rolls; this will be noticed in such surnames as ' Couper' written ' Coup,' ' Shepherd' as ' Shep.'

In certain styles of mediæval writing the terminals of words are carried upwards with a long sweep, and are confusing in their resemblance to abbreviation marks. Here, again, practice alone accustoms the eye to decide whether a word is complete or not.

Dots and other kinds of stops in writing have only come gradually into use in their present significance.

In the Anglo-Saxon manuscripts, as in Roman inscriptions, the dot is freely used to denote contractions as well as to divide the words from each other. In Domesday this is also noticed; but with later manuscripts the dot, or point, such as is used in Norman times, fell into disuse in favour of lines or curves for the abbreviated syllables. Upon the introduction of printing our various kinds of stops are first observed. It is said that the Elzevirs invented some of them. The reversed semicolon is commonly observed in some manuscripts.

Sooner or later, in any antiquarian search, the printed sources of information will be exhausted, and are not unfrequently found to be untrustworthy, especially county histories, which, being compiled by men unacquainted with every minor detail of the locality, are naturally liable to confuse places of similar names. Nor is it possible in so large a subject as a county history to enter minutely into the separate parish histories of places and people. Thus after awhile the untrustworthiness and insufficiency of book-knowledge will be discovered, and some more original source of information become desired. Manuscripts exist in plenty, but are of little value unless studied personally; for professional readers, although able to read quickly and correctly, only give the information desired; whereas in a personal search one subject opens out fresh clues to others of equal importance, and new light is continually being thrown upon hitherto unnoticed points; moreover, only by a personal investigation can the antiquary be certain that he has obtained exactly what he required. There are now plenty of opportunities open to the public of seeing the old documents pertaining to various offices and societies, besides private collections, but without some previous knowledge of the old handwritings, etc., this permission is practically valueless. Therefore, ' Persevere and practise ' is the best motto I can give to those interested in the matter, for proficiency comes quickly to those who seek it; and, as in all subjects, ' Nothing ucceeds like success.'

THE END.